The
Shipwreck
Cannibals

ADAM NIGHTINGALE

The Shipwreck Cannibals

CAPTAIN JOHN DEANE
AND THE
BOON ISLAND FLESH EATING SCANDAL

The
History
Press

To Matthew Frost, God's adventurer.

Cover: *Shipwreck*, Alexey Bogolyubov, 1850

Internal illustrations by Stephen Dennis and Jean Nightingale
Photographs by Mark Nightingale, Carol King and Adam Nightingale

First published 2013

The History Press
The Mill, Brimscombe Port
Stroud, Gloucestershire, GL5 2QG
www.thehistorypress.co.uk

British Library Cataloguing in Publication Data.
A catalogue record for this book is available from the British Library.

ISBN 978 0 7524 8723 6

Typesetting and origination by The History Press
Printed in Great Britain

Contents

Acknowledgements

y thanks go to the following, whose assistance, tip-offs, encouragements and crash pads contributed to the writing of *The Shipwreck Cannibals*: Peter Nightingale; Susannah Nightingale; Alec and Jo Cobb; Gio Baffa; Nigel Brown (the Sheriff of D Block); Margaret Kight; Paul Baker; Carol King; the staff of the National Archives; Mark Beynon, Lindsey Smith, Lauren Newby and Cate Ludlow of The History Press; John Pycroft and the staff and pupils of Emmanuel Church of England School; Bromley House; Warren Weiss; and Richard Warner, whose original research provided the skeleton to which I added the succulent meat.

What shall we do unto thee, that
the sea may be calm unto us?

The Book of Jonah

Introduction

*O*f the ten survivors of the *Nottingham Galley*, Captain John
Deane was one of the few that could still physically stand
upright when a New England fishing boat retrieved him and
his crew from the rock the locals had christened Boon Island. The
fishing vessel, or shallop, had left the open sea and had entered the
mouth of the Piscataqua River on the way to Portsmouth where
food, lodging and medical attention awaited Deane and his crew.

There had been fourteen survivors when the ship had struck rock
and marooned the crew on Boon Island. Four had died. Two had
perished on the island and one was lost to the ocean. The body of the
last of the dead had been discovered on the mainland. The rest had
survived for twenty-four days blasted by the wind and soaked by the
ocean, with no natural shelter and virtually nothing to eat. They had
come close to starvation. They had come near to madness and had
believed themselves eternally damned. They had all done something
to survive that they were loath to talk about away from the confra-
ternity of survivors. They had eaten human flesh.

John Deane's credit was good and he was keen to get to his lodgings ahead of the rest. He had arranged for a canoe to take him to
Portsmouth faster than the shallop could presently manage. Deane
transferred from the shallop to the canoe. He took his friend Charles
Whitworth with him. Whitworth was lame in both feet and incapable of walking. He had to be carried into the canoe. The two
men reached shore at eight o'clock in the evening. Deane spotted his lodgings and leapt out of the canoe. He forgot himself for a
moment. He had barely strength enough to walk but now he ran to
his lodgings. He entered the house unannounced. He was skeletal.

His hands were torn ragged and some of his fingernails were missing. The house belonged to Jethro Furber, a friend of Deane's who had led the party that had rescued him and his crew from Boon Island. As Deane entered the house unannounced he encountered Thurber's wife and children who fled from him in fright.

Deane seemed indifferent to the fact that he had driven his hosts from their own home. He walked around the house until he found the kitchen. He picked out the ingredients for a meal, some turnips and some beef. He placed them on the kitchen table, determined to cook something for Mr Whitworth and the men that had rowed him here. He began to prepare the meal. He reserved a small piece of turnip for himself and ate it raw.

Preparations for the meal were disrupted when a group of local men entered the kitchen. They laid hands on John Deane and dragged him from the kitchen table. Confusion reigned for a short while until Mrs Thurber returned to the house with more accurate information. John Deane was released, taken to his room and tended to. Mr Whitworth was lifted from the canoe and carried to the Thurber house.

The remaining survivors of the *Nottingham Galley* were brought to Portsmouth and taken care of by the town's populace. Most of them were incapable of walking. Most had suffered horribly from frostbite. Only John Deane retained possession of all of his fingers and toes. Many of the survivors would never regain full health. A few would die shortly afterward.

The men convalesced as best they could. The town seemed to take them to heart. It was evident that a great drama had played itself out some seven leagues from where they lived. The survivors were rendered heroes in the eyes of the populace. But it couldn't last. At some point the protest, the official account a captain must give when he has lost his vessel, had to be written. The shared secret needed to be addressed. They had all eaten human flesh. They had done it to survive. They had eaten a man already dead. No innocent blood had been shed. But any potential scandal Deane must have anticipated was all of a sudden subsumed in a new controversy.

Deane wrote his protest. Christopher Langman, the first mate, countersigned it. But as soon as he was well enough to leave his lodgings Langman turned on his captain. Along with the boatswain Nicholas Mellin and George White, a member of the crew, Langman appeared before a local magistrate and all three signed affidavits denouncing John Deane. They accused Deane, his brother Jasper and Charles Whitworth of fraud. They claimed that Jasper Deane and Charles Whitworth had overinsured the ship's cargo and that John Deane, on at least two separate occasions, had tried to lose the ship so that Jasper Deane and Charles Whitworth might claim on the insurance. The second attempt to lose the ship had resulted in the wreck of the *Nottingham Galley* and the subsequent loss of four lives. Langman, Mellin and White also accused John Deane of having perpetrated a violent assault on the first mate in the hours immediately preceding the shipwreck.

Little seemed to have been done to address the accusations in New England so Deane and company, and Langman and company, returned to the British Isles and resumed the controversy there. In London, John Deane got wind of the fact that Langman intended to publish a detailed account of the Boon Island adventure. Jasper Deane quickly rushed into print Deane's version of events, narrowly beating Langman to the punch. A pamphlet war erupted. And although accusations of fraud and brutality were the principle charges for each side to either prosecute or refute; tales of cannibalism were the salacious anecdotes lapped up by the reading public that turned the affair into a *cause celebre*. And although both parties agreed on the necessity of eating human flesh in their warring versions of events, each put their own spin on theirs and their enemies' attitudes towards cannibalism.

Everyone involved would be tainted by the events of Boon Island. But because John Deane lived the longest and achieved the most, the weight of the broken taboo hung heaviest upon him. And despite a career that would bring him into the orbit of Peter the Great and Robert Walpole, heaping glory and further shame upon him, the spectre of Boon Island would always cling to him, like Sinbad's Old Man of the Sea, wrapped around his throat and waist, choking him, virtually impossible to dislodge no matter how hard he tried.

Part One

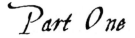

Survivor

Two Brothers

John Deane was born in either 1678 or 1679. His older brother was named Jasper after their father. He had a sister named Martha. The family was moderately wealthy. Other than that, virtually nothing is known of Deane's youth and early adulthood. His childhood home was the village of Wilford. The parish of Wilford was situated on the southern borders of Nottingham. Nottingham Castle was visible across the River Trent and the fields that separated Nottingham from Wilford Village. The dark, compact Anglican beauty of St Wilfrid's church dominated the river bank on John Deane's side of the Trent. Access to Nottingham was granted by ferry. In land-locked Nottinghamshire the ferry would have been John Deane's principal contact with the element of water in his early years.

By the time John Deane was ready to embark for New England, Nottingham was still the modest conurbation that Daniel Defoe would describe in the 1720s as, 'one of the most beautiful and pleasant towns in England'. Wilford was a benign satellite to the pleasant East Midlands town. Although subject to the rigours of an eighteenth century quasi-pastoral existence that included unnavigable roads, punishing winters, flooding, poaching and the occasional act of highway robbery, Wilford was a relatively pleasant place for John Deane to have grown up in. The only real emblem of the chaotic world beyond the county's borders was the presence in Nottingham of a prisoner of war, the French aristocrat Camille d'Houston, the Comte de Tallard, captured at the Battle of Blenheim and residing in the town under luxurious house arrest.

The biographical void of John Deane's early years would become filled with tall tales. John Deane was a butcher's apprentice. He fell in

with a gang of professional deer thieves. He left the gang for fear of
the gallows but the itch for excitement remained. He sought satisfaction through legalistic channels and joined the Royal Navy. He fought
against the French in the War of Spanish Succession. He prospered
under the martial governance of Admiral Rooke. He was present at
the liberation of Gibraltar. He was promoted to the rank of captain.
He left the navy but by 1710 was broke and in need of a financially
rewarding venture that would satisfy his taste for high adventure.
He threw in with his brother and decided to go to New England.

Apart from the friends and business contacts the Deanes had clearly
established in New England, and a reference in a letter John Deane
wrote in the late 1720s to having been in the coastal Irish town of
Dungarvan 'at the beginning of the late French wars', virtually nothing of the elaborate prequel to the events of 1710 can be substantiated.
Most of it came from the imagination of the forgotten Victorian writer
W.H.G. Kingston, author of a popular novel about John Deane. Many
of the fanciful imaginings of Kingston's fiction were reported as fact
by Victorian and Edwardian historians and still exist as corruptions in
the biography of John Deane to this day. Whatever the true nature of
John Deane's naval apprenticeship, his brother Jasper certainly felt confident enough in his abilities to offer him the captaincy of a small ship
in a trade voyage to the English colonies on the east coast of North
America. Jasper Deane had gone into partnership with the merchant
Charles Whitworth. He had bought a 120-ton ship. He named the ship
the *Nottingham Galley*. Its cargo of rope and cheese was jointly owned
by Jasper Deane and Charles Whitworth. A crew was recruited and
plans were made for a late-season voyage to Boston in 1710.

The *Nottingham Galley* may have originally been Swedish, a prize
taken in war and then sold on to Jasper Deane. Its ten guns were
certainly Swedish. If the vessel itself wasn't from Sweden then the
guns may have been fitted onto an unarmed English vessel, weapons on a merchant ship being a necessity even in times of peace as
attack from pirates was a constant threat. But England was still at war
with France and the coastal waters were fertile hunting grounds for
Louis XIV's privateers.

Half of the *Nottingham Galley*'s cargo was in London. The other half was in Ireland. To get there the *Nottingham Galley* would have to sail the long way round the British coast in order to minimise the chance of encountering the French. This was not the only risk. The lateness of the season meant a greater chance of storms and bad weather.

In August 1710 fourteen men set sail for New England. What follows is John and Jasper Deane's version of events.

2

The Captain's Story

ohn and Jasper Deane's account of the voyage began as they approached the Irish port of Killybegs to pick up their cargo before setting sail for Boston. Prior to this, as Langman's account would attest, they had set sail from Gravesend in early August and sailed to Whitby under the protection of a merchant convoy guarded by two men-of-war before Deane had broken away from the convoy and sailed to Killybegs. Between the shore of the mainland and the island of Arran, as they approached Killybegs from the south, they spotted two ships heading toward them. The ships were French privateers.

Langman would make much of Deane's encounter with the privateers, accusing him of deliberately trying to secure the ship's capture. John Deane, in his account, didn't mention the privateer episode at all. The Jasper Deane-sponsored account gave it short shrift, stating that John Deane's intentions, should the *Nottingham Galley* fail to outrun the French, was to run the ship aground and torch her rather than submit to capture.

The privateers were successfully evaded and the *Nottingham Galley* docked in Killybegs. Deane's cargo was a mixture of rope, which he had taken on board in London, and butter and cheese, which was waiting for him in Ireland. Three hundred pieces of cheese and 30 tons of butter were loaded onto the *Nottingham Galley* at Killybegs. The ship set sail for Boston on 25 September 1710. Nothing dramatic happened of any significance until the *Nottingham Galley* approached New England in early December.

Land was spotted. The *Nottingham Galley* was east of the Piscataqua River, heading south toward Massachusetts Bay. The coast of New

England was covered in snow. A north-easterly gale assailed the *Nottingham Galley* with hail, rain and snow. A thick fog enveloped the ship and the mainland was obscured from view. The fog hung on the ocean for approximately twelve days. Around the eleventh day the fog lifted for fifteen minutes. In that tiny window of visibility John Deane observed the mainland and tried to determine where they were. Neither Deane nor his crew could make any kind of accurate judgement as to their exact position; 'unaccountable currents' had dragged them off course. Nevertheless John Deane ascertained that the safest course of action would be to steer the ship in a south-westerly direction because the wind was blowing in from the north-east and land lay to the north-east and the south-west. His intention was to sail south-west until ten o'clock that evening and then lie by until daybreak the following morning. It was the eleventh of December, or thereabouts.

The weather was against them. The *Nottingham Galley* was peppered with further rain, wind and snow. John Deane had posted a member of the crew as a lookout. Deane stood watch himself. The time was somewhere between eight or nine o'clock at night. Through the evening black, John Deane spotted waves breaking where there shouldn't have been waves. He called instructions to the steerman to, 'Put helm hard a starboard!' The command caught the steerman by surprise. The steerman bungled his orders but it made no difference. The command had been issued too late. The *Nottingham Galley* had struck rock.

The impact was violent and disorientating. The waves were high and the night so dark that whatever the ship had hit was barely visible through the black. The crew couldn't stand upright on deck. The ship was lifted by the waves and swung parallel with an island that none of the crew could yet see. Waves broke across the deck. John Deane ordered his crew to take immediate shelter in his cabin. Fourteen men huddled together below deck. John Deane called his crew to prayer for their immediate deliverance. Once they had offered up pleas to God, John Deane set them to work. He ordered his men back on deck. He commanded them to chop down the masts. He led by example.

Some, but not all of the crew, followed him. Those that stayed behind had temporarily lost their nerve, paralysed by the fear of death and the prospect, despite their prayers, of imminent eternal damnation.

The wind, for the only time that night, aided John Deane and his crew. The force of the gale snapped the masts before Deane and company could do any real damage to them. The ship's masts fell toward the mass of rock barely discernible in the dark. A crew member risked his life by climbing onto the bowsprit and trying to see what it was exactly that the ship had struck. He was the first to make out the small land mass and reported his observations to the captain. The masts had formed a bridge and a possible route of escape, should the hull of the ship be breached. Deane summoned Christopher Langman, the first mate. He called on Langman because he was a strong swimmer. Deane selected two more equally skilful swimmers and gave them the task of reaching the rock and finding the safest place for the remainder of the crew to join them. Once Langman and company had found a safe point of disembarkation they were to alert Deane. Langman and company shimmied across the masts toward the rock. Deane returned to his cabin.

John Deane had gone back to the cabin in order to retrieve anything that might have been of value to the crew if the ship sank. He was looking for official papers, money and the means to make a fire, namely gunpowder and a flint. He was making provision for the dual prospect of either being marooned or rescued. Deane descended the steps below deck and entered his cabin. As he began gathering his things the ship lurched and the stern sank deeper into the ocean. The walls of the ship bulged inward. Seawater entered the ship at a frightening rate. Deane had underestimated the damage that had been done. The spine of the *Nottingham Galley* had been shattered and she was drowning in salt water. Deane grabbed what he could and struggled to get back on deck. It was a near call. He had come dangerously close to drowning in the belly of his own dying vessel.

Nothing had been heard from Christopher Langman or the two swimmers that had accompanied him, so John Deane decided to traverse the fallen mast himself and try and reach the rock. He removed his outer clothing. He waited for the movement of the sea to carry the ship that bit closer to the rocks and then climbed onto the mast. The mast was predictably slippery but Deane moved forward as best he could. He reached the end of the mast. The mast didn't quite

Captain John Deane crossed the broken mast of the *Nottingham Galley* in order to reach the precarious safety of Boon Island. *Illustration by Stephen Dennis*

touch the rocks. Deane would have to jump the gap and hope that he could gain purchase on the rocks without injuring himself too badly. Deane jumped. He reached for the rocks but the rocks were slippery. He slid into the freezing water. He was lifted by the sea and flung back against the rocks. He found it hard to gain purchase. He struggled to climb to a safe part of the island. He would make a small amount of progress and then fall back in the ocean. As he hung onto the rocks, as he repeatedly tried to drag himself up and onto the island, the rocks cut into his fingers and ripped out some of his fingernails. Eventually Deane hauled himself to a place of relative safety and coughed up and spewed out the salt water he had taken into his lungs.

Deane shouted back to his men. He guided them across the mast and onto the island. All the remaining crew members reached the island in safety. Deane and the ten men whose rescue he had just engineered walked across the island seeking higher ground. They met Christopher Langman and his two companions. It was ten o'clock in the evening. All fourteen men huddled together and prayed, thanking God that they were all still alive.

Deane and his crew travelled leeward looking for any kind of natural shelter. There was none to be found. As they walked, the dimensions and character of the island were becoming clearer to them all. The island was a scant 100 yards long and 50 yards wide. Besides rockweed there was virtually nothing in the way of vegetation. The ground was a mass of jagged rock. The simple act of walking was painful. The sharpness of the rocks also negated the only way, at present, they had of keeping warm, the stone prohibiting walking around to generate warmth and protect their circulation. Deane and his crew were forced to huddle together, motionless, their only defence against the wet and cold on their first night on Boon Island.

Deane began his first morning on Boon Island with a degree of optimism. If the night's labours had been principally concerned with abandoning ship and keeping his men warm and alive, then the morning was to be about salvage, rescuing whatever he could find from the broken corpse of the *Nottingham Galley* and using the provisions to sustain his men until rescue.

Deane made his way to shore. He expected to see much of the ship still skewered on the rocks. But there was virtually nothing there. The bulk of the *Nottingham Galley* had been carried away and buried by the ocean. Masts, yards and detritus floated on the water, secured by the ship's anchor. This was nature's taunt to Deane and his men, as the wreckage was at the mercy of the waves and too far out to sea to safely retrieve. Bits of tent, wood, canvas and sail had washed up on the shore or else could be found in the rocks. At present these were the only materials Deane had to work with. They would have to do.

Most of the food had gone down with the ship. Fragments of cheese were found among the rockweed. Added together they amounted to the equivalent of three whole pieces of cheese. Even rationed carefully they wouldn't last long. Gulls circled the island and floated on the water. Seals were spotted nearby but not on shore. The island was presumably their home so it could only be a matter of time before one of them ventured onto land and sacrificed itself to the needs of an already hungry crew. During his stay on Boon Island, John Deane would make frequent midnight hunting trips to capture a seal. He never did. But there were more pressing needs than seal or gull meat. The men required a fire. Between them they had a flint, some gunpowder and a drill. For the next ten or so days they would repeatedly try to utilise these tools to start a fire. Their efforts would prove useless. Their materials and everything around them was irredeemably sodden.

Two gunpowder horns had been rescued from the *Nottingham Galley*. These became the crew's water receptacles. One was designated for common use among the men. One was reserved for the sick. On Boon Island there was always rain enough to provide a steady source of fresh drinking water. There was enough snow and ice on the island to provide a secondary source of water, although the snow and the ice had a predictably salty tang to it. However desperate things would get, the absence of drinking water would never be a serious impediment to their survival. It was one of nature's few concessions to Deane and his crew in the painful ordeal that lay ahead of them.

At the end of their first full day on Boon Island the men tried to sleep. Their situation had been fractionally improved by a canvas sheet that had washed up on shore. They crawled underneath it and huddled together.

On the morning of the second day the elements had improved somewhat. Up until now, any view of the mainland had been obscured by the hostile weather. It was still frosty but John Deane could see land and had an inkling of where they were. He believed that he was looking at Cape Neddock. It was fishing country and so the chances of being spotted by a shallop improved the possibility of rescue. At least that was what he told the men. Privately he was doubtful that any shallop would risk the winter sea to sail close enough to the island to ever spot them. He kept his doubts to himself but let his men dine for a while on the succulent half-truth, good morale being as valuable as food, water or warmth at this point in their endeavours.

It seemed to be a time of introspection for John Deane. He was concerned with questions of command now that a form of de facto equality had fallen on the marooned crew. Aboard the *Nottingham Galley* his authority had been absolute. He would have expected his orders to have been obeyed without question. Deane had been on the island for less than a few days and some of the crew had refused simple requests as well as direct commands. Crew members were shirking the common tasks. Deane's response was to neither impose command nor insist on obedience. He wandered off alone to search for materials, a pretext designed to give the crew the necessary room to decide for themselves if they still wanted him to lead them. The crew talked in Deane's absence. The majority came to the decision that Deane would remain their captain; that they would defer all powers of command to Deane exactly as they had when on board the *Nottingham Galley*. Ten men were in agreement. There were three voices of dissent, the first mate Christopher Langman and two unnamed sailors. Langman and company were overruled.

John Deane was made aware of the crew's decision. He agreed to carry on as before with the concessionary gesture of consulting the crew in the case of certain important decisions.

The next few days on Boon Island were spent searching for further materials and tending to the sick. Three crew members had fallen ill. They all convalesced together. Worst among them was the ship's cook. He was physically weaker than the rest of the men and inexperienced when it came to toughing out the natural rigours of life at sea. In these extreme circumstances it was more than his body could bear. At noon, on the third or fourth day, the crew reported the cook's death to John Deane. Deane ordered the cook's body to be taken to edge of the island and given to the waves.

When the cook had been alive he had been the most conspicuous in his complaints about the lack of food on Boon Island. He seemed to feel the extremities of hunger before anyone else. The other crew members hadn't arrived at that point of desperation quite yet. But as the cook's body was given to the ocean many privately considered whether his corpse might not have been put to better use as a meal for the living. These were the first thoughts of cannibalism among the crew. Even John Deane was not immune, pondering privately whether it might not have been better to eat the dead cook rather than bury him at sea.

The supply of cheese had not yet run out. There was about half a pound of cheese for each man. During the food distribution Deane would ensure that everyone received exactly the same ration. This was an act of diplomacy on Deane's part. Despite the crew's decision to obey Deane's orders, not everyone appeared to be pulling their weight in the allocation of daily tasks. Deane could have withheld food from those he deemed to be wilfully lazy but he chose not to.

In that first week on Boon Island, in addition to the cheese, the crew ate powdered bone. The bones were from pieces of beef from the food supplies of the *Nottingham Galley*. Fish had eaten the meat but the bones had washed up on shore. The crew smashed the bones to powder on the rocks in order to render them digestible.

The men were starting to show the grotesque physical effects of half a week in the freezing wet. Most of the crew were suffering from frostbite. Many had lost some degree of feeling in their fingers and their toes. When fleeing the *Nottingham Galley* some members of the crew had gone barefoot. Others had worn boots and stockings. Those that wore boots had to have them cut from their feet. As the boots were removed and the stockings peeled off, skin and toenails came away with the material. Feet were horribly blistered. Deane tended to the wounds of his men as best he could. He personally dressed ulcers, binding feet in makeshift bandages fashioned out of linen, rags and oakum that had washed up on shore. He cleaned wounds, washing them with an antiseptic brew concocted from a mixture of seawater and human urine.

The hands of many of the crew had begun to change colour. This was a source of pressing concern for Deane. Discolouration presaged the onset of mortification. It was important to keep the blood circulating in the hands and feet, or fingers and toes might have to be amputated. The best defence against the mortification of the skin was work. And there was important work that needed to be done. The canvas sheet could not continue as their only defence against the night cold. A shelter had to be constructed. Building work would be easier than had been previously anticipated as carpenter's tools had been discovered in the preceding day's search for materials.

The first structure built by the survivors of the *Nottingham Galley* was a tent. It was triangular in shape. The tent was between 8 and 9ft in diameter. It was made from a mixture of canvas and sail and bits of oakum. The tent pole was a wooden staff. On top of the pole was a flag made out of a piece of cloth that stood as a signal to passing vessels. It was an important achievement but there was a problem. When it came time for the men to bed down for the night it became evident that there wasn't enough space within the shelter for everyone to lie down properly. All of the crew were obliged to sleep on their sides. Problems arose whenever a single crew member decided he wanted to turn over. If a man turned over it caused disruption among the other men. Deane's solution was to regiment the men's sleep. During

The crew of the *Nottingham Galley* took shelter from the fierce New England elements in an improvised tent. *Illustration by Stephen Dennis*

the night, at two-hourly intervals, a call would be given and the entire crew would turn over in unison. Comical though it must have appeared, it seemed to work and the men's chance of getting some approximation of rest was substantially increased.

Deane and the crew began to turn their attention to getting off the island. Having built a tent they now felt galvanised enough to try their hand at constructing a small boat. In terms of materials there was now sufficient wood washed ashore to build a boat. Nails had been discovered in the rocks. As far as tools were concerned the men had a caulking mallet and a cutlass. Many of the crew had their own knives. They used the knives to carve teeth into the cutlass blade, turning a weapon into an improvised saw.

John Deane described his crew's efforts:

> Three planks were laid flat for the bottom, and two up each side, fix'd
> to stanchings, and let into the Bottom timbers, with two short Pieces
> at each End, and one Breadth of new Holland's-Duck round the
> Vessel, to keep out the Spray of the Sea: they caulk'd her with Oakum,
> drawn from old Junk: and secured the Seames with Canvas, Pump-
> leather, and sheet-lead, as far as the extent of their small Stock would
> allow; a short mast was fix'd, with a square Sail; seven Paddles provided
> for Rowing, and an eighth, longer than ordinary, for Steering.

While constructing the boat the workforce consisted of John Deane
and two members of the crew. A working day lasted four hours. The
cold prohibited working any longer than that. On some days the cold
was so intense that no work was done at all. The irony of the entire
endeavour was that the man best qualified to oversee the building of
the boat was too incapacitated to help. The ship's carpenter was so
weak he couldn't even offer advice. He had been among the first of
the survivors to fall ill. He coughed up large amounts of phlegm and
suffered from back pain and neck stiffness. He would lose the use of
both feet and be incapable of walking.

At the end of that first week on Boon Island three things happened that raised the crew's morale: work was finished on the boat;
a carpenter's axe washed up on shore; and three boats were spotted.
John Deane was the first to spot the boats. They were about 5 or
so leagues away. They were sailing from the south-west. The wind
was north-east. Most of the crew were in the tent. John Deane
called them all outside. They shouted and gesticulated trying to get
the attention of the boats. The boats didn't see them and sailed by.
The crew ought to have been despondent but instead drew encouragement from the near miss. They reasoned that the boats might have
been a search party responding to the presence of wreckage from the
Nottingham Galley that had washed up on the shore of the mainland.
If this were the case, then an ongoing search must be in progress and
rescue was simply a matter of time.

In spite of a newly acquired incentive to sit where they were and wait for rescue, most of the crew were still determined to use their newly constructed boat and affect their own deliverance if they could. Work had finished on the boat around about 21 December. The day's weather was relatively placid and favoured an attempt to launch the boat. There was space in the boat for six people. Which six was a point to be debated by Deane and the crew. Deane proposed himself. The crew agreed. Deane was the fittest among them and the most experienced. It was also agreed that Jasper Deane and Christopher Langman should go. Four more crew members whose names are not reported were selected. The crew paused for a moment's prayer, committing the success of their impending adventure to God.

Every crew member that had the strength to do so dragged the boat to the water. The crew were weak. Dragging the boat was an effort. The sea was uncharacteristically smooth. The surf was high. The boat was dragged into the water. The crew were obliged to wade deeper into the sea than felt safe to ensure that the boat was properly launched. John Deane and a crew member hauled themselves into the boat first. The smoothness of the ocean was deceptive. There was a sudden swell in the water that turned the boat over and pitched Deane and his companion into the sea. The boat was smashed to pieces against the rocks. The carpenter's axe and the caulking mallet had been on board. Both tools were lost to the ocean. Deane and his companion struggled to get ashore. Both men nearly drowned in the attempt.

Deane and the crew were despondent. The blow to their morale erased all thoughts of discovered wreckage and New England rescue parties. As if to mimic their mood, a violent storm blew up that afternoon. John Deane drew some encouragement from the tempest. He knew that, had his boat not capsized, he would be in the ocean in the middle of the storm and would surely be dead. He saw something of the wisdom and the grace of God in the destruction of the boat. He also believed that God had spared him for the sake of the men. He remained the fittest among them and possessed the soundest mind. The men relied on him. If he died then they would not know what to do. They would give up. Deane's sense of divine perspective was not shared by his men. That night their melancholy could not be penetrated. They truly believed that they would all die on Boon Island.

Boon Island exacted its toll on the survivors in increments. Their physical condition was growing worse by the day. The hands of many of the crew were starting to exhibit symptoms of gangrene. Ulcers were giving off a shocking odour. There was nothing left to bind the wounds with, save a bit of linen rag. And at last hunger had supplanted lack of heat as the main impediment to Deane and his crew's chances of survival. The supply of cheese had run out. Deane scoured the island for alternate sources of food. The men ate rockweed and kelp. Deane found mussels, which the men could eat raw, but they were physically difficult to gather. Nevertheless, Deane managed to provide his men with an average of three raw mussels a day.

Although hunger was their greatest enemy there were other devils to contend with. Those who understood the seasons knew that there was an impending spring tide due. The tide could theoretically cover the island and drown them all. Concerns of a more metaphysical nature assailed the minds and the souls of many of the crew. With death as tangible as it was, some of the men feared that if they died they would go straight to hell. The prospect of eternal punishment invoked a profound and debilitating fear among the crew. John Deane was more certain of his own standing with the Almighty. He believed that God had blessed him with more physical strength, a better constitution and a stronger mind than his crew specifically for the purpose of exhorting and encouraging them to trust in the delivering power of God.

Deane and the crew's attempts at piety manifested itself in a strange relationship with the calendar. During the course of their stay on Boon Island, no member of the crew was ever completely certain what day of the week it was. In recounting the events of Boon Island, both John Deane and Christopher Langman often approximated the dates when recalling their experiences. The crew would observe two Sundays during the week, presumably out of a sense of religious anxiety, making certain that they accurately observed the Sabbath, even if that meant observing it twice. They also celebrated Christmas Day on two separate occasions, just to be certain.

The crew needed something to galvanise them to activity. John Deane had given Christopher Langman the job of trying to trap and kill a seagull. While they had been on Boon Island the seagulls had floated on the water and flew by but had seldom landed on the rocks. If Langman could trap and kill one, the fresh meat might provide the necessary spur to move the men to work. Langman killed his seagull. He presented the dead gull to John Deane who cut it into thirteen pieces and distributed it among the men. There was barely enough for a mouthful each. The meat was raw but the men were grateful and enjoyed their tiny meal. It was a small difference but it had the desired effect. The men's spirits lifted and they were ready for their next great endeavour, the building of a raft.

The crew member at the heart of the new building project was a man known only by his nationality. John and Jasper Deane simply called him the 'Swede'. The only physical description of him is that he was 'stout'. John Deane would express doubts and a degree of ambivalence about the success of the venture he was about to bring into being. In contrast, the Swede would completely embrace the prospect of building a raft and became the main motivating force behind its construction. In fact, since arriving on Boon Island, it had been the Swede that had repeatedly suggested the prospect of building a raft as a means of escape. The mood of the group was in accord with that of the Swede. Construction began on the raft.

What made the Swede's involvement truly remarkable was the fact that he could not walk. Since his arrival on Boon Island, the Swede had contracted a severe case of frostbite in both feet. He quickly lost the use of his feet and became one the crew's first invalids. Although not explicitly stated, it is likely that the Swede was one of the two stricken crew members obliged to convalesce with the dying cook. He was an excellent swimmer and may have been one of the two men selected to accompany Christopher Langman when he left the *Nottingham Galley*. The Swede had suffered more than most but his enthusiasm was infectious. A new optimism seemed to arrest the crew.

It took five or six days to build the raft. The crew had virtually no tools at hand and limited raw materials. John Deane described the raft's construction:

> After deliberate thoughts and consideration, we resolved upon a Raft, but found abundance of labour and difficulty in clearing the Fore-Yard (of which it was chiefly to be made) from the junk, by reason our working hands were so few and weak.
>
>   That done, we split the Yard, and with the two parts made side pieces, fixing others, and adding some of the lightest Plank we cou'd get, first spiking and afterwards seizing them firm, in the breadth of four Foot: We likewise fix'd a mast, and of two hammocks that were drove on shore we made a sail, with a paddle for each man and a spare one in case of necessity.

The raft was only big enough to carry two men. The Swede insisted that he was to be one of the two. He wanted John Deane to accompany him. This time Deane refused. He didn't share the Swede's confidence in the mission's chances of success. The nature of the raft's primitive construction would leave the occupants waist-deep in water while trying to either sail or row to the mainland on a journey that would take a minimum of ten to twelve hours. Deane had also been here before. His own experiences in the first shattered boat can only have informed his pessimism. But for the sake of the rest of the crew, at least for the time being, Deane kept his misgivings to himself.

There must have been an unwelcome sense of déjà vu when shortly after construction was finished on the raft another boat was spotted. This time the sail of a ship was seen. The ship was leaving the Piscataqua River some seven leagues away. Once again the crew attempted to get the attention of the ship. The ship failed to notice them and the ever oscillating mood of the crew sank back into a familiar despair.

The following day the crew called on their depleted reserves of optimism and endeavoured to launch the raft. The weather was reasonable but it was afternoon, somewhat late in the day to safely attempt something like this. The Swede had found a replacement for John Deane and was keen to set sail. Christopher Langman cautioned the Swede to launch at another time. Langman stressed the lateness of the hour as reason not to sail. The Swede reassured Langman that an afternoon launch made no difference as it was a full moon that night and as far as he was concerned that was as safe as sailing in the daylight. John Deane agreed. The crew prayed together and the raft was launched.

Like Deane before him the Swede and his companion were tipped into the ocean by another swell. The Swede was an outstanding

A swell in the ocean tipped the Swede into the freezing sea as he tried to escape Boon Island in a makeshift raft. *Illustration by Stephen Dennis*

swimmer and made it back to shore. His companion floundered and went under. John Deane swam after him and dragged him to safety.

The men retrieved the raft before it could be smashed against the rocks. The raft was intact but the mast and the sail were gone. The Swede was keen to get back in the raft and try again. This time Deane cautioned against it, advising patience for a better opportunity to relaunch the raft. The Swede didn't want to wait. He was kneeling on the rocks. He grabbed his captain's hand. He conceded that he might die but he was determined to go anyway. He wanted John Deane to come with him but was willing to go alone if necessary. He asked Deane to help him back into the raft. Deane was reluctant. He pointed out the obvious; that without the sail and mast the journey would take twice as long and the chances of survival would be greatly reduced. The Swede was adamant that he needed to attempt the journey. He hated Boon Island and would sooner drown in his raft than stay there any longer than he had to. Deane consented and gave the Swede permission to relaunch the raft.

The Swede's first sailing companion would not rejoin him but the Swede's example moved another member of the crew to take his place. John Deane gave the Swede some money. It was estimated that the Swede would reach the mainland at two o'clock in the morning. If successful his instructions were to light a fire on a designated hill in the woods as a signal that he had reached the shore safely. The Swede was helped back onto the raft. He requested the remaining party pray for him as long as they could still see him. The Swede and his new companion rowed and steered the raft toward the mainland. The crew watched and prayed until they couldn't see the Swede, his companion, or the raft anymore. As the raft disappeared from view it was estimated that the Swede was halfway to shore. During the evening the good weather evaporated and the wind grew rough and violent.

Two days after the Swede had left Boon Island the crew saw smoke rising from the mainland. The smoke came from a different position than that agreed between the Swede and his crew mates. Yet the crew still believed that the author of the smoke signal was the Swede. If the Swede and his companion had made it to the shore then they would find settlers and bring help. The Swede appeared to have fulfilled his part of the bargain. The onus on the crew was to stay alive until help arrived.

The threat of the spring tide had passed. Boon Island had not been covered with water as feared. Nobody had drowned but the water level had risen bringing with it a more subtly dangerous set of problems. The water submerged the mussels John Deane had been harvesting. The mussels were now the men's main source of nourishment. Deane still tried to ensure that his men received their daily ration of three mussels each. Deane took it upon himself to collect the mussels because he was still the strongest man among the crew and because the men refused to do it themselves. The majority of the men were either incapacitated, unable, or simply loath to help. To collect the mussels Deane had to repeatedly sink his hands into the icy cold water. Each time he did this his hands went numb for a while. The longer he did this the more he risked permanently losing the feeling in his hands and arms. Gangrene might follow and if that happened, Deane would have to have his hands amputated to stop the rot spreading to the rest of his body. The irony of the entire venture was that whenever Deane tried to eat a mussel himself he couldn't keep it in his stomach. He ate rockweed instead.

The crew waited. As the anticipated rescue failed to materialise, it became evident that the prospect of starvation was now the men's principle adversary. The men still believed the Swede was alive. They believed that the rivers on the mainland had frozen. They rationalised that this had delayed the Swede's attempts to find a settler with a boat that might come and retrieve them. They would wait for the Swede. They would do whatever was necessary to avoid starving to death.

A piece of main yard washed up on shore. Attached to it was a patch of green hide. The men wanted to eat it. They pleaded with their captain to bring it to them. Deane retrieved the hide, cut it into tiny pieces and let the men feed on it.

Although Deane was stronger than the rest he was feeling the stab of hunger in his own tortured fashion. He considered eating the ends of his own lacerated fingers. He considered eating his own bodily waste.

Deane tried to keep his men active as best they could manage. If they were reluctant to leave the tent then they could mend it.

The health of two members of the crew was of particular concern. Deane's cabin boy seemed particularly susceptible to the cold. Deane tended to him with an extra degree of care. At night, Deane and the boy removed their wet clothes. They wrapped themselves in oakum and Deane bid the boy lie on him to share body heat. But the most stricken member of the crew was the carpenter. At this stage in his illness he couldn't talk. He could only communicate through drawing. He was too weak to cough up the large deposits of phlegm that hung heavy upon his lungs. The crew tended to him as best they could. He died sometime in the night, his corpse resting among the sleeping members of the crew until morning.

On the first full day of the carpenter's death, John Deane instructed the stronger members of the crew to remove the corpse and place it a safe distance from the tent. Deane left the tent to look for food and supplies. He found another piece of hide attached to another piece of the main yard. He picked the hide up and bit into it, testing its suitability as food. It was tough and his teeth couldn't make any kind of purchase on the rough material. Around noon he returned to his men. The body of the carpenter was still in the tent. The men hadn't lifted a finger to shift it. When Deane asked why, the men complained that they were too weak.

Deane was incensed but tried to contain his anger. He searched around for some rope. He gave the rope to the men and ordered them to tie it around the carpenter's body. Deane took hold of the rope and tried to drag the corpse out of the tent. He was weaker than he thought and found the labour difficult. He was joined by a few other members of the crew but their combined efforts were feeble. They dragged the body a few steps outside the tent and then gave up.

John Deane returned to the tent exhausted. He wanted to sleep but there was something wrong with the crew. There was an intensity among them and an alertness present that had been absent in recent days. Charles Whitworth needed to talk to Deane in front of the men. He told Deane that the crew wanted to eat the body of the carpenter.

While Deane had been out foraging, the crew had discussed what to do with the carpenter's body. They had elected Whitworth as their spokesman because he was a gentleman and more likely to persuade the captain to consent to their request. John Deane said nothing. He was appalled. The crew pleaded with him to let them eat the carpenter's body. When Deane finally spoke, it was to organise a conference of sorts that would debate and discuss all the moral permutations of what they were proposing to do.

Deane did his best to hide his exhaustion. He listened to arguments and counter-arguments. There was the dual consideration of legality and theology. What they were doing might be illegal, unnatural and sinful; a crime against the law of the land, nature and God himself. Weighed against that was the necessity to survive. Nobody really knew if the Swede had been successful in his endeavours or whether he was in fact dead. If he was successful, the crew couldn't guarantee that they could sustain their existence long enough on infrequent meals of raw mussel and patches of hide for a rescue party to reach them before they starved to death. Deane listened to all the arguments and decided to put it to the vote.

The decision to eat the dead body was by no means a completely unanimous one. Despite their hunger, Christopher Langman and two others were strongly opposed to cannibalism on religious grounds. But the majority voted 'yes' and Deane gave his consent to butcher and eat the dead body of the carpenter. The majority were ecstatic.

Deane tried to reassure Langman and his allies. Nobody had killed the carpenter. The need to survive was arguably the greater moral imperative. To eat his corpse was only wrong if the crew had been complicit in ending his life for that purpose. That had not been the case. They had tried to keep him alive as long as possible. No sin had been committed. Langman was not convinced and Deane, despite being an apologist for cannibalism in those moments, almost certainly retained some degree of doubt. But once the decision had been made, he committed to the practicalities of what they were about to do. Deane reasoned that, despite the levels of hunger, the reality of eating raw human flesh might be more difficult for the men than they had anticipated. He decided that human flesh needed to look like animal meat. It would be an easier adjustment for the men to make when the time came. In order to do this, any physical semblance of humanity in the carpenter's corpse would have to be cut away and dumped into the sea. What was left would be quartered, dried and divided into rations, which Deane would control. The majority agreed but the question remained as to which of the crew would help with the butchering.

None of the crew would consent to help butcher the body. When Deane wanted to know why, the crew complained that it was too cold to work, or that they were sickened by the actual mechanics of butchery and couldn't do it, despite an academic willingness to join in. Deane was angry and offered no assistance. The crew begged him to butcher the corpse. Deane eventually agreed. He managed to persuade one member of the crew to join him and the bloody work began.

Deane and his companion cut off the carpenter's head, hands and feet. They skinned him. They extracted his bowels. They threw the sundered body parts and rejected internal organs into the sea. They cut strips of flesh from the carcass and washed them in salt water. By the time the sun had set, they had their first ration of the new meal.

Deane brought the strips of meat back to the tent. He leavened the meal with rockweed and distributed the ration among the men. Christopher Langman and the other two dissenters refused to touch the meat. The rest of the crew devoured the flesh with great enthusiasm. John Deane's first taste of human flesh was a gristly piece of meat from the carpenter's breast. He could barely keep it down.

The following morning Langman and his two companions gave in and received their ration. John Deane took to calling the rations 'beef' in his belief that the men might still need some form of semantic bridge to help them make the adjustment to eating human flesh. He needn't have concerned himself. The men took to their new diet with a gusto that disturbed their captain. Two days later, Deane had real cause for alarm. Once the men had tasted the carpenter's flesh they craved more of it. Deane had taken advantage of the crew's general level of physical incapacity and his own superior constitution.

He had moved the supply of flesh further away from camp, to a sharp and difficult part of the island, hard for anybody but Deane to get to. He controlled the men's rations despite their demands for more.

Deane feared that cannibalism would accelerate the chances of ulcerated and mortified skin. These fears ran concurrent with increased concerns about the state of his own torn fingers. But it was the new meat's effect on the men's characters and personalities that really alarmed him. The men were wilder. Their eyes blazed. They argued more than they had done. They refused orders. There was a brutish air about them. The once unifying institution of corporate prayer dissolved among the men as a previously binding and comforting discipline. The men swore and blasphemed openly. There was a greater burden on Deane to protect and ration the supply of flesh. He feared that once it was exhausted, the stronger men would kill the weaker men and eat their remains. In those moments John Deane regretted not having given the entire body of the carpenter to the sea.

On New Year's Day the men were a sorry mess of ulcerations, numbness, gangrenous wounds and broken spirits. Charles Whitworth was now lame in both feet. Men couldn't feel their fingers. Their physical inertia was interrupted by violent spasms. Blasphemy had increased among some, while others feared that these last miserable moments of their freezing existence were about to be supplanted by an eternity burning in the fires of hell. John Deane was nearly finished. He had some strength left but his faith was at its lowest ebb. He was tired of caring for these men.

On the morning of 2 January John Deane left the tent. He was the first to do so that morning. He looked out across the sea. There was a shallop on the water. The shallop was equidistant between the island and the mainland. The shallop was sailing toward Boon Island. John Deane shouted, 'A sail! A sail!' The men left the tent as best they could, their mood altered in a matter of moments from despair to joy.

As the crew of the shallop sailed their vessel nearer to Boon Island, John Deane became more visible to them. He waved his arms to get their attention. He walked across the island signalling the best place to weigh anchor. The crew of the shallop saw Deane clearly enough but didn't comprehend his meaning. The shallop dropped anchor south-west of the island, 100 yards away, remaining in its position until noon. The sea at present was too dangerous to risk coming any closer. Deane's men struggled to master their own mood, fearing another deferment.

The afternoon brought with it kinder waters and the shallop moved closer to Boon Island. Deane and the crew of the shallop were now within shouting distance of each other. Deane told the New Englanders most of what had happened to him and his crew since the shipwreck. He made a point of not mentioning that the survivors were in want of food. The implication of Deane's omission was that if supplies were delivered to the island then it might become evident what Deane and the men had had to do to avoid starvation. There was no way of predicting how the fishermen might respond to that knowledge. It was best, in Deane's eyes, to avoid difficult questions for the time being.

The one thing Deane did request was the means to make a fire. The crew of the shallop agreed and dispatched a man in a canoe. The canoe reached Boon Island safely and Deane helped drag it ashore. The fisherman, standing face to face with John Deane, couldn't speak for a moment. He was shocked to silence by Deane's emaciated form and wasted appearance. Deane asked him questions and the man found his voice. Deane wanted to know what day it was. He wanted to know about the Swede.

The fisherman didn't know anyone called Swede. Someone had found the remains of a raft on the mainland shore. They had found a dead man on shore, frozen solid with a paddle tied to his wrist. It wasn't the Swede. The Swede, whoever he was, must have been lost to the ocean. But the presence of the raft meant a shipwreck and the prospect of survivors. The local government had been moved to send a search party to seek out the marooned.

Deane led the fisherman across Boon Island toward the tent. On the way, the fisherman spotted a pile of raw meat on the rocks. He expressed pleasure that the survivors had had a ready source of food to eat during their ordeal. John Deane agreed but didn't elaborate on the true nature of the meat, allowing the fisherman to walk to the tent comforted in his ignorance.

Once again the fisherman was stunned when he saw the physical state of the rest of the men. He helped them to build a fire and then talked to John Deane about how best to get them off the island. It was agreed that Deane would return to the shallop with the fisherman in the canoe. Then the canoe would come back, the plan being to empty the island of survivors one or two at a time. John Deane climbed into the canoe and nature's black comedy played itself out once again when a wave forced the canoe into a rock and John Deane and the fisherman went into the sea. Deane barely had the strength to swim back to shore. The canoe was retrieved. It was relaunched but without Deane. The fishermen promised to return the next day if the weather wasn't too dangerous. The shallop sailed back toward the mainland.

The sky turned black. A storm blew up. The storm lasted the night and the length of the next day. Nobody came back for Deane and his men that day. It was too dangerous to sail. The survivors' spirits were low but the fire made a difference.

The fire was never to be left unattended. At any time, during the day or night, two or three of the crew were given the task of feeding and stoking the flames. But to begin with the fire was more of a hindrance than a blessing. There wasn't any kind of vent for the smoke within the tent. The men had failed to pre-empt this and asphyxiated themselves until a tear could be made in the roof to let the smoke out. The other obvious benefit of the fire was cooked food. That evening the carpenter's flesh was broiled and the men had their first hot meal on the island. Cooked flesh inflamed the men's desire for more. Deane was pragmatic. He increased their ration in the hope that it would sate the men's hunger somewhat.

During the night John Deane was lying on his side, unable to sleep. Two members of the crew were tending to the fire. They were talking in a furtive manner. Deane couldn't hear what they were saying but inferred mischief by the tone of their conversation. One of the two men crawled out of the tent. He returned with a piece of carpenter's flesh and began to cook it in the fire. John Deane erupted. He grabbed the meat and publically denounced both men before the rest of the crew who had been rudely woken up by the violent disturbance. Deane was angry. He was fully intent on punishing the thieves. But his fury seemed to dissipate as soon as it had risen and he merely reprimanded them instead.

On the morning of 4 January some kind of moral semblance seemed to have reinforced itself in the routine of the men. The men were praying when their devotions were interrupted by the sound of a gunshot, a musket fired into the air to get their attention. Deane and the men left the tent. A shallop was anchored near the island. A canoe disembarked from the shallop. Aboard the canoe were two friends of John Deane: Captain William Lang, an Englishman; and Captain Jethro Furber, a native of New England. The captains were accompanied by three more men. The weather was good enough to effect a rescue.

In comparison with the drama of Deane and company's trilogy of abortive attempts to leave Boon Island, Lang and Furber's rescue was comparatively mundane in its efficacy. It took two hours to transfer the crew from the island to the shallop. Talking with his rescuers it became evident to Deane that, had the survivors left with the fishermen on 2 January, they might not have survived. During the storm the shallop had struggled to get back to shore. But the fishermen got word to the authorities in Portsmouth who had made haste to get to Boon Island as quickly as they could.

John Deane was taken aboard the shallop first. The rest followed in twos and threes. Many of them had to be physically carried onto the boat.

On board the shallop, on the way to Portsmouth, the survivors were given a bit of bread to eat and a dram of rum to drink. It was a deliberately small ration followed up a short while later with a bowl of gruel. The sea took a rough turn. The men threw the gruel up. The effect of the vomiting was twofold. It cleansed the men's stomachs but also intensified their hunger. The crew of the shallop, for health's sake, had to take extra care to control their guests' intake of food, now that food was more freely available.

The shallop sailed up the Piscataqua River. It docked at Portsmouth. The men were delivered into the care of the locals. There were numerous amputations of gangrenous toes and frostbitten fingers.

Once they had convalesced awhile, the crew members that weren't directly embroiled in the feud that was to flare up between Deane and Langman drifted off, 'some sailing one way and some another'.

5

The First Mate's Tale

What follows is based on Christopher Langman, Nicholas Mellin and George White's version of events.

The *Nottingham Galley* sailed from Gravesend on 2 August 1710 with a cargo of rope.

Christopher Langman was displeased with the state of the ship. Four of the ten guns didn't work and of the fourteen-man crew, Langman would claim that, 'not above six were capable to serve in the ship, in the case of bad weather.'

On 7 August the *Nottingham Galley* joined a convoy of merchant ships headed for Scotland. The convoy was protected by two men of war. The *Nottingham Galley* enjoyed the safety of the convoy until Whitby. A gale blew up. The convoy refused to sail during the bad weather. Captain John Deane left the convoy, deciding to chance it and made for Ireland where he was to pick up the rest of his cargo.

On 21 August, off the coast of Ireland, John Deane was standing watch. He spotted two ships, three leagues distance from the *Nottingham Galley*. The ships were waiting in a bay to the leeward of Dean's vessel. He called Christopher Langman on deck. Deane told Langman that he wished to sail toward the two ships. Langman and other members of the crew observed the vessels and perceived that the ships were probably French privateers. To obey the captain's orders was to risk capture. They advised a more evasive course of action. John Deane repeatedly made his wishes clear: approach the ships. The crew refused to obey his orders. Deane did nothing.

Nicholas Mellin and George White overheard Charles Whitworth talking to John Deane. Whitworth admitted that he had rather the

Nottingham Galley be captured by the French. Whitworth owned an eighth of the ship. He stated that he had insured the ship to the sum of £200. The implication was that the money that could be made on the insurance, should the vessel be taken, was a greater financial enticement than selling the cargo in New England. John Deane admitted that his brother Jasper had had exactly the same thoughts, having paid £300 in insurance. John Deane stated that if he could get away with running the ship ashore and claiming the insurance money then he would do so. It is unclear in Langman's account and the subsequent affidavits whether this conversation took place during the night, during the following day, or whether the conversation took place twice. But all three of the crew members that would later sign the affidavits were united in the conviction that John Deane, his brother and Charles Whitworth intended to deliberately lose the *Nottingham Galley* for criminal profit.

In the morning the privateers were spotted again. John Deane repeated his intention to sail toward them, or else weigh anchor and allow the French to approach the *Nottingham Galley*. John Deane was supported by his brother and Charles Whitworth. Once again Langman and the crew opposed their captain. John Deane changed tactics and bid the men sail toward the shore. At some point in the morning Deane ordered Nicholas Mellin to hoist the *Nottingham Galley*'s tackle over the side of the ship, a precursor to going ashore. John Deane and Charles Whitworth went into the cabin. They collected their valuables and put them in a chest. They ordered the chest to be moved to a rowing boat. Then Deane assured his men that they 'should want for nothing'. It was a tacit bribe to enlist their support in what he was preparing to do. John Deane intended to run the ship aground.

Once again, Christopher Langman refused to obey John Deane's commands. He explained to Deane that the *Nottingham Galley* was only 7 leagues from its destination. The wind favoured them. They could outrun the privateers and be in port and safety before nightfall. Langman would not sail the ship any closer to shore than was absolutely necessary. Deane let the first mate have his way. Langman navigated the *Nottingham Galley* safely between the shore of the Irish coast and a nearby island evading the privateers and arriving in the port of Killybegs sometime between six and seven o'clock in the evening.

The *Nottingham Galley* stayed in Killybegs for the rest of August and most of September. Thirty tons of butter was loaded aboard the ship as well as three hundred cheeses. On 25 September 1710 the *Nottingham Galley* set sail for Boston.

As a captain, John Deane's conduct off the coast of Ireland had been extraordinary. He had attempted to take a course of action flagrantly designed to effect either the capture or the loss of his vessel when alternative means of escape were available. He had also given orders that had been refused and hadn't disciplined his crew for what was effectively mutinous behaviour. For better or worse, a captain's authority needed to be absolute in the hermetic commonwealth of an ocean-going vessel. But now that Deane and his crew were in the open sea the captain reasserted his authority with a vengeance. He began a campaign of systematic abuse. He beat the men. He singled out two crew members that had been particularly conspicuous in their opposition during the privateer episode. He beat them so badly that they couldn't work for an entire month. He weakened the men by reducing their rations, allowing them a single quart of water per day. To exacerbate their thirst, he fed them salt beef. To sate their thirst, whenever it rained, the crew were driven to virtually lap water from the ship's deck.

On one particular occasion, John Deane forgot to lock the hold that permitted access to the ship's water supply. An unnamed member of the crew discovered the captain's error. He stole below deck. He took a gallon of water. His intention was to distribute it among the crew and give them a decent drink. John Deane interrupted him. He hit the man hard, knocking him to the ground. Many of the crew thought, for a few moments, that John Deane had killed their shipmate.

Deane's actions had no pragmatic value to them. He had re-established his authority, but in doing so had also physically weakened his crew. The motives for his actions appeared to have had more to do with revenge for the earlier usurpation of his authority and the spoiling of his scheme than anything else. Deane's violence and the crew's inability to withstand it attested to something about Deane that his own, his brother's, and his enemy's testimonies all agreed on: John Deane was a physically tough man. His constitution could endure more punishment than his peers, if Deane's and his brother's accounts are to be believed. He could also dish out brutal physical punishment without fear of retaliation, if Langman and company's testimonies are to be believed. Even taking this into account, the crew's passivity seems a little bit extraordinary. John Deane had his brother Jasper and Charles Whitworth to support him but they were not particularly tough men. The crew's passivity becomes more understandable when we know that John Deane had access to at least one firearm. And before the voyage was done he would use his gun to threaten the life of Christopher Langman, the only crew member still capable of defying the increasingly unstable captain.

As the *Nottingham Galley* approached Newfoundland, a ship was spotted sailing toward her. The ship appeared to be in pursuit of the merchant vessel. John Deane and Charles Whitworth's previously grim mood changed with the news. They were both suddenly agreeable and generous. They opened the ship's store of grog and gave the men free reign to get as drunk as they pleased on brandy and strong beer. Deane and Whitworth both believed that the new ship was another privateer. To receive their captors, Deane and Whitworth changed into their best clothes. They were mistaken. The ship was the *Pompey*, an English vessel.

As the *Nottingham Galley* sailed on to New England, the first land spotted was Cape Sables. Boston was 50 leagues away. John Deane lay the ship by for a few days. This was the process in which a ship would stop sailing in order to avoid bad weather or else administer repairs. The weather was reasonable. When Deane set sail for Boston, the weather was starting to become more troublesome, strong enough to necessitate the furling of the ship's sails to avoid them being shredded by the wind. A westerly wind forced the ship off course. The *Nottingham Galley* lost sight of land.

Between seven and eight o'clock in the morning, on 11 December, Nicholas Mellin spotted land. The land was situated leeward of the *Nottingham Galley*: Cape Porpus. Mellin called the captain and the first mate to the deck. Almost as soon as the two men were brought together they began to argue. John Deane claimed that the land Mellan had spotted was the first land that they had sighted. Langman disagreed. They had spied land a week previously when they had passed Cape Sables. The argument must have seemed, for a moment, like a fatally mistimed exercise in one-upmanship between two master pedants. But there were consequences to Deane's lapse of memory that Langman felt compelled to point out. The *Nottingham Galley* was currently too close to shore. The *Nottingham Galley* had strayed off course precisely because Deane had decided to lay the ship near the very Cape Sables he currently couldn't remember having seen. Deane's delay had caused the ship to hit the bad weather that had blown them off course; he was responsible for their current situation. Deane's actions had cost them a week. Had they carried on at Cape Sables then they would, in Langman's estimation, be in Boston by now. As it stood, they were unnecessarily delayed and too close to the shore.

The discussion was now an argument from which the crew seemed to draw a form of moral strength that favoured Langman. Deane appeared to concede the argument. He walked away and went below deck to fetch the men their water ration. Deane distributed the water and went down into the ship's hold. Christopher Langman was drinking his ration from a bottle. Jasper Deane approached Langman, took the water bottle from him and struck him with it. John Deane emerged from the hold, carrying a wooden periwig stand. Langman was stunned from the bottle attack and, in those moments, unable to defend himself properly. John Deane hit Langman across the head three times with the wooden block. Langman collapsed. He lay on the deck and didn't move. Blood ran from the wounds in his skull soaking Langman and the deck around him red. The crew thought that Langman had been murdered. Now they would do whatever John Deane ordered them to do.

Langman survived the assault. He was taken below deck to his cabin, physically damaged and temporarily silenced. He remained there for twelve hours as the situation above him deteriorated. The weather was turning hostile. The ship was being forced towards the mainland. John Deane was back in command and unopposed.

John Deane attacked Christopher Langman with a periwig stand hours before the *Nottingham Galley* struck rock at Boon Island. *Illustration by Stephen Dennis*

In the early evening Nicholas Mellin realised that the *Nottingham Galley* was far too close to shore. He alerted the captain but also told Christopher Langman. The first mate walked onto the deck. Covered in his own dry blood, Langman challenged Deane for the second time that day. He stated that Deane had no right to be so close to the shore unless it was his express intention to wreck the *Nottingham Galley*. Langman counselled Deane to 'haul further off', to sail against the wind rather than let it blow the galley further inland.

Deane told Langman that he would not listen to him, even if it cost him the ship. Deane threatened Langman. He told Langman that he would get his pistol and shoot him. Then Deane told his men that he would 'do what he pleased except they confined him to his cabin'. The captain was throwing down a gauntlet. He was instructing his crew to go ahead and mutiny if they had the courage to do so.

John Deane didn't shoot Christopher Langman. The crew didn't mutiny. A weird stasis seemed to fall on the captain, the first mate and crew of the *Nottingham Galley*. John Deane was in his cabin preparing for bed when the ship struck Boon Island.

As the *Nottingham Galley* came apart on the rocks John Deane apologised to anybody that would listen. He told his crew to prepare themselves for death as any hope of escape was futile. Many of the men tried to make their way onto the deck of the ship but breaking waves forced them back below. Deane began to weep and howl like an animal but other members of the crew were trying to determine the extent of the damage and see what could be done to save their companions. Nicholas Mellin went below deck to see if the hold had been breached. The hold was letting in water. Mellin returned to the cabin and gathered the men around him. They prayed to God that the ship might keep together until morning.

Christopher Langman stood on the deck. He tried to assess what needed to be done. He was physically weak but the drama of the occasion seemed to give him energy and strength. Langman went to see John Deane in his cabin and rebuked him for demoralising the men. Deane told Langman that it was useless, all of them were going to die. John Deane, who under normal circumstances was either inept, corrupt, or else a despotic lunatic, was now completely neutered as a source of effective leadership. Langman elected to take charge.

The *Nottingham Galley* was taking in water at a disturbing rate. Anyone on deck was in danger of being knocked into the sea by the breaking waves. Despite these hazards, and the added element that it was virtually impossible to stand upright on deck, Langman and three others began to chop down the fore-mast and the main-mast, hoping to form a bridge between the island and the ship.

John Deane was still in his cabin. Christopher Langman paid him another visit. He implored Deane to think of his men and how he might save them. Deane was more preoccupied with retrieving anything of value before the ship went down. Langman left Deane alone and went back on deck.

Langman was first onto the makeshift bridge. He crossed the bridge to the shore of the new island. He encouraged others to follow him. Three men took his lead. The rest of the crew remained behind. Langman and his compatriots seemed to disappear into the black as they crawled across the sundered mast. They could not be seen through the darkness of the evening or heard above the din of the ocean. The remaining crew could not tell if any of the four men had reached the shore or had been swept into the sea. They were divided in their minds as to whether to stay or cross over. John Deane wished to stay. The crew prayed. The decision was made for them. The cabin began to take in water. The men were forced onto the deck, obliged to crawl on their hands and knees. A couple of men braved the mast and bid the rest follow them. Having no choice all the remaining crew members of the *Nottingham Galley* crossed the bridge and reached Boon Island in relative safety.

Every man was soaked. Their clothes were heavy and waterlogged. There was no shelter. They feared that the high tide would cover the island and drown them all. They expected to die that evening. They prayed. They thanked the Almighty. They confessed their sins to God. If they could survive the night then there was a degree of hope.

The men expected the main bulk of the *Nottingham Galley* to be intact and reasonably accessible, in which case goods could be salvaged and their chances of survival improved. During the night a man was sent to look for the *Nottingham Galley*. He returned and reported that there was nothing there. The ship had disappeared. Morning came. The island had not been swamped by the tide as the men feared. All fourteen members of the crew were alive but the *Nottingham Galley* was gone. The only evidence that it had ever existed was bits of wreckage washed up on the shore.

Among the wreckage was half a cheese caught up in a piece of the ship's rope, some linen and some canvas. The cheese was distributed among the men. The linen and canvas was used to make a tent. Nicholas Mellin oversaw the tent's construction. By the second day the tent was finished and habitable. Christopher Langman credited the tent with saving the crew from freezing to death but it couldn't keep out the wet. The tent's present location posed a danger. The tent had to be moved to higher ground to avoid the tides that covered that part of the rock. The tent provided some protection but little comfort. When the men slept they slept on stones. Despite the new shelter, keeping warm would be a problem. The jagged topography of Boon Island prohibited walking around as a means of improving the body's circulation. The tent failed to save the ship's cook who died of exposure. The crew grieved. Their mourning seemed to be an amalgam of genuine sadness for a fallen shipmate and a lament for themselves as they feared that they too would freeze to death before long. The crew removed the cook's body from the tent and let the sea have him.

The weather improved and the men drew some inkling of where they were. They were three or so leagues from the mainland. The sight of the New England shore gave them hope. If they were so close to civilisation then rescue was a realistic possibility. But the new knowledge brought its own set of frustrations. It was evident to Langman that the *Nottingham Galley* could have avoided hitting the island had they steered west by south. The storm would have blown them onto the shore of the mainland.

There was enough wreckage to build a boat. Cold and hunger had drained the men of much of their strength but they worked at their new task regardless. The boat was 12ft long and 4ft wide. It could hold six men. Canvas was used to waterproof it. It had no sail. It was a crude construction but as ready to make its maiden voyage as it would ever be. The question remained as to who would man the boat? Many of the crew pleaded to be the first to go. The matter was discussed. The carpenter had built the vessel and had earned the right to go. In spite of his previous conduct it was adjudged that John Deane also had the right to go. Nicholas Mellin was chosen because he could speak the language of the native Indians. The rest were Jasper Deane, Charles Whitworth, George White and Christopher Langman, one man more than the prescribed six the boat was thought capable of holding.

The plan was simple. The boat was to reach the shore and those onboard were to get help. The carpenter would take his tools with him in case they needed to build a better vessel when on the mainland. The boat was launched. The keel turned upwards and the seven men were pitched into the sea. They swam back to the island with difficulty. Some nearly drowned. Nicholas Mellin had hold of the boat by a rope. The ship's gunner grabbed the rope. The two men hung on to the rope for an hour. They hoped to keep hold of the boat until the sea settled and then they would retrieve it. As the two men held on to the rope the ocean slammed the boat into the rocks again and again until nothing remained but splintered wood. The carpenter's tools sank to the bottom of the ocean. The destruction of the boat was hard on the men's morale but they prayed anyway and thanked God for the safe delivery of the seven men who had tried to row to the mainland.

Snow fell on Boon Island. The wind grew fierce. The clothes of the men that had survived the destruction of the boat began to freeze about their weakened bodies.

The following day the weather improved. The shore could be seen with greater clarity than at any time since the shipwreck. Houses were visible. Boats could be observed rowing from one place to another.

The crew were jubilant. They prayed that they might be spotted and rescued. They stood at what they perceived to be the key points on Boon Island where they would be most visible to the people on shore. They shouted to get their attention. They were too far away to be heard.

The men were hungry. They subsisted on small rations of cheese. There were four or five bits of beef to share as well as a calf's tongue. The food supply was finite. More food needed to be found. George White discovered a part of the island where raw mussels could be harvested when the tide was low. He collected two or three days' worth, which amounted to six or seven per day for each man. The crew thanked God for the new source of food. But it was often difficult to sustain the supply because of the high tides and the cold weather. The flow of fresh mussels was arrested almost as soon as it had begun. John Deane had something to say about it. He continued his rolling Jeremiad, advising the crew to 'shift for our selves, there being nothing now for us to trust to but the mercies of God'. The crew ate seaweed. A piece of cow's hide was found. It was cut into small pieces and the men chewed on it.

The morale of the crew started to lift. Even John Deane was making prudent suggestions about how he could contribute to the men's wellbeing, should they ever be rescued. He said that he would sell any of the cannons, cables and anchors of the *Nottingham Galley* that had washed up on shore and would use the money from the sale to pay for his own and the crew's care and upkeep.

Morale was given a further lift when Christopher Langman discovered a seagull sitting in a hole in a rock. He killed the seagull with the handle of a saucepan. The seagull was divided and distributed among the crew who ate the bird flesh, like everything else they had consumed on the island, raw.

A grim realisation fell upon the crew. Help was not going to come from the mainland. They had to effect their own deliverance. A 'stout Dutchman' proposed the notion of building a raft from the remaining wreckage. He even volunteered to be the first to man the raft if no one else wanted to risk the journey.

The raft was made from the remains of the fore yard of the *Nottingham Galley*. All of the work was carried out by a weak crew with virtually no tools. They stripped the rigging. They split the yard in two to make the sides of the raft. A plank constituted the raft's middle. A sail was improvised from two hammocks.

The Dutchman would be first to man the raft on its maiden voyage but there was room for a second person. George White elected to accompany the Dutchman. Their task was get to the mainland, find help and light a fire as a signal to the men on Boon Island that they had arrived safely. The launch was a failure. The raft was overset. The Dutchman and George White were tipped into the sea. They managed to get back to the island but nearly drowned in the attempt. The raft was retrieved. The Dutchman was undeterred and wanted to go again but the sea had knocked all defiance out of George White. A nameless volunteer, a Swedish man, put himself forward and the raft was relaunched. The crew watched the raft until sunset. It appeared to be on course, near enough to the shore to give the men hope.

There was a hard wind that evening. During the night the carpenter died.

In the morning, members of the crew dragged the body of the carpenter out of the tent. John Deane and Christopher Langman had gone foraging for food. They returned empty-handed. John Deane was first to propose the notion of eating the carpenter. Deane reasoned that God had permitted the carpenter to die. The men had not been complicit in his death therefore it was not a sin to eat the corpse. Deane volunteered to butcher the carpenter but needed assistance. He asked Nicholas Mellin if he would help but the boatswain was too feeble. A crew member named Charles Grey assisted Deane. Between them Deane and Grey removed the carpenter's head and hands. They skinned him. They put the head, the hands and the skin somewhere close by. They butchered the carcass and brought the first helpings of the new meat ration back to the men. With the exception of Christopher Langman, Nicholas Mellin and George White, the crew ate the carpenter's raw flesh. The three abstainers lasted until morning and then, caving in to hunger, accepted their ration.

John Deane dismembered and butchered the corpse of the *Nottingham Galley's* carpenter. Eating the dead carpenter's flesh kept the surviving members of the crew alive while they waited to be rescued. *Illustration by Stephen Dennis*

For the most part the men's response to consuming human flesh was measured. The majority refrained from eating too much as they were unsure how it would affect their health. John Deane did not appear to have the same concerns and ate more flesh than any other member of the crew. As he did so, he grew more abusive and argumentative, as did Jasper Deane and Charles Whitworth. John Deane's piety diminished in proportion to the amount of flesh he ate. He stopped praying with the rest of the crew and cursed and blasphemed to such a degree that Christopher Langman felt compelled to upbraid him for 'profane swearing'.

The thoughts of the crew turned back to the Dutchman when smoke was spotted rising from the mainland. They believed that he had been successful. They reasoned that rescue was imminent.

On the evening of the twenty-first day on Boon Island, Christopher Langman dreamt that a sloop would come for them. The dream was so vivid that Langman took it to be prophecy. In the morning he sent the ship's gunner to look and see if the dream had any substance. The gunner saw a sloop sailing toward Boon Island. The crew were ecstatic. They offered up prayers of thanks to God.

The sloop weighed anchor as near to Boon Island's shore as was safe. It was too dangerous to attempt a landing. The survivors of the *Nottingham Galley* shouted to the sloop and asked if those on board might help them start a fire. The sloop dispatched a solitary man in a canoe. He brought with him the means to make a fire but that was all. There were no other provisions. When the rescuer saw the survivors at close proximity he was afraid of them, such was their ragged and ghoulish appearance. The crew surrounded him and in unison began to vocalise their joy at finally being discovered. Through the rescuer the crew learned the fate of the Dutchman and his companion. The raft had been found on the shore of the mainland. A single frozen body had been discovered nearby under a tree. The rescuer reasoned that the man in the raft had come ashore during the night and had died because he was ignorant of the area and did not know where to go to find assistance and shelter. The body of the second crew member had not been found and was presumed lost to the sea.

John Deane was supposed to return to the sloop but the canoe overset and Deane fell into the water. It was shallow this time and he was able to wade back to shore. The crew of the *Nottingham Galley* picked up the canoe and carried it across the island to find a better place for it to return to the sloop. The solitary rescuer stayed with the survivors for three hours. When he left them it was with a promise to return better equipped and get them off the island.

A storm blew up. The sloop struggled to get back to the mainland. The sloop sank. The crew of the sloop made shore by the skin of their teeth. The captain of the sloop sent a communiqué calling for assistance for the men still stranded on Boon Island. For the crew of the *Nottingham Galley* the force of the storm was leavened by the presence of fire. After almost a month of murderous cold, the heat of the fire must have felt glorious. The carpenter's flesh certainly tasted better now that it could be broiled.

The bad weather continued throughout the next day. There was no rescue party. That night the men decided to foreswear their ration of cooked flesh. They abstained for fear that if their rescuers came the next morning they might abandon them if it became obvious what the crew of the *Nottingham Galley* had done to survive. It was a shrewd decision. The following day the rescue party arrived. The survivors could finally go home.

The evacuation from Boon Island was overseen by a Captain Long and a Captain Forbe. The men were transferred from Boon Island to the awaiting vessels. Many had to be carried as the freezing cold had wrought havoc on their limbs and they could not walk. Christopher Langman commended the care and attention shown to the survivors by Captain Forbe and Captain Long. The two captains ensured the survivors were fed but controlled their intake of food. The rescue party arrived at their destination at night. John Deane stayed in lodgings belonging to a Captain Purver. The crew were looked after by the locals. A doctor was assigned to the survivors. Christopher Langman and George White suffered from diarrhoea and fever. The frozen flesh of the cabin boy's foot had mortified. Part of the foot had to be cut away to stop the gangrene spreading to the rest of the cabin boy's body. In spite of their terrible afflictions the men were glad to be alive. Christopher Langman praised the care and attention of the locals. He attributed his own and his crewmates' survival to the 'goodness of God'.

A few days into the survivors' convalescence, John Deane wrote his protest. He brought the protest to Christopher Langman and George White to sign. Both men were sick and dependent on the care of the locals for their health and wellbeing. They were physically weak and vulnerable. They didn't want to sign the protest but were afflicted by a renewed fear of Captain John Deane. Now that he was back on the mainland among his peers and friends, Deane was in a powerful position to exert his influence to Langman and White's detriment if they refused to comply with his wishes. Both men believed that John Deane would have had them evicted from their lodgings if they failed to endorse his account of the loss of the *Nottingham Galley*. Langman and White signed the protest.

John Deane's behaviour on the mainland was cruel and irrational. Deane was the channel through which the relief of the townspeople passed. It was down to Deane to disseminate the relief to the rest of his men. He abused the trust placed in him. He hogged the best of the relief for himself and his brother Jasper. According to Langman, a Captain John Wentworth 'gave several of our men good clothes,' but 'Captain Deane came and ordered them the worst that could be had'. To compound the vicious treatment of his ailing crew, John Deane had his men evicted from their lodgings before they were fully recovered.

John Deane did not seem to be in complete control of his own vindictive moods. Prudence ought to have necessitated that Deane showed a more benevolent side to his friends and deliverers than he did to his crew, but Deane seemed incapable of concealing his cruel nature. He did not exhibit any obvious gratitude for his rescue and he mortally offended his host. While talking with Captain Purver's children, Deane told them that 'he would have made a frigasy of them, if he had 'em in Boon Island'. Captain Purver threw his guest out.

Once Christopher Langman, George White and Nicholas Mellan were well enough, each man wrote an affidavit accusing John Deane of fraud and of having perpetrated a violent assault on Langman. On 9 February 1711, in front of their own captain, the three men swore to the veracity of their statements before a justice of the peace.

4

$\mathcal{E}$ighteenth-Century Rashomon

y 1711 the events of Boon Island had become a talking point in London. It was known that Christopher
Langman intended to write an account of the shipwreck exposing John Deane, Jasper Deane and Charles Whitworth
to public disgrace. As rumours began to circulate, before anything
had yet appeared in print, John and Jasper Deane were already subject to hostile treatment. Charles Whitworth had died shortly after
the Boon Island incident and was spared much of the humiliations
meted out to his friends. Jasper Deane complained that he and his
brother were subject to 'daily ignominious scandals, and injurious
mobbing to our faces'. Necessity demanded that Jasper begin work
on his own account of the shipwreck. A race was on to see which of
the two factions would get their version of events into print first.

Jasper Deane beat Christopher Langman to the punch. *A Narrative
of the Sufferings, Preservation and Deliverance of Capt. John Dean: in the
Nottingham Galley of London, Cast Away on Boon-Island, near New
England, December 11, 1710* was published in the summer of 1711. Jasper
Deane's account was drawn from an expanded narrative written by
John Deane from which Jasper 'omitted many lesser circumstances'
that would 'swell this narrative beyond its design, and thereby exceed
the bounds of common purchase'. Jasper Deane set down what the
'design' of his narrative was to be in the introduction to his account:

> A few months past. I little expected to appear in print (especially on
> such occasions) but the frequent enquires of many curious persons (as
> also the design of others to publish the account without us) seem to
> lay me under an absolute necessity, lest others acquainted, prejudice

the truth with an imperfect relation. Therefore, finding myself obliged to expose this small treatise to public view and censure, I persuade myself that what's here recorded will be entirely credited, by all candid, ingenious spirits; for those whose kind opinion I am really solicitous.

Jasper Deane presumed that those who knew his brother would believe the account. He gently challenged those who were doubtful of John Deane's integrity to seek out such Boon Island survivors that were presently in London and ask their opinion. Jasper Deane described the prose style he had adopted for his account as 'smooth' and 'unaffected' without 'unnecessary enlargements ... relating only matters of fact.' He made reference to others who had read it, approved it and insisted that it be published. He praised the New Englanders that had nursed the crew of the *Nottingham Galley* back to health. He made mention of those who had already read his narrative, their verdict being that it was 'novel and real'.

Despite being known as Jasper Deane's narrative, the story was told in the first person from John Deane's point of view. The encounter with the French privateers off the coast of Ireland was not mentioned. The narrator relayed the details of the storm and the shipwreck. In these moments John Deane was presented to the reading public as a courageous and pragmatic man, overseeing the escape from the damaged vessel but having the foresight to retrieve from his cabin what might be useful on the island. Deane's near fatal journey from ship to shore resulting in the loss of his fingernails, the first few days on Boon Island, the attempt to build a shelter and the onset of hunger and physical decay were all described. In the middle of the narrative John Deane stood astride the chaos, an unassuming and occasionally introspective leader who led by example. Christopher Langman and company were neither named nor criticised. The initial attempts to construct a boat were relayed in relatively forensic detail. The attempt to launch the raft offered the first explicit mention of Christopher Langman. Simply referred to by his rank, Langman was mentioned in the context of volunteering to be one of the first to sail in the boat. It was a tacit acknowledgement of a positive quality in Langman, his courage.

The aftermath of the boat's destruction portrayed John Deane interpreting the event in the context of God's providential mercy. The captain's piety was a recurring theme in the Jasper Deane account.

The next few pages concerned themselves with the various attempts to fend off hunger and the construction of the raft. Again, Langman's contribution was positive, hunting and killing the seagull that provided the crew of the *Nottingham Galley* with a much needed infusion of meat into their diet. The Swede took centre stage, supplanting both John Deane and Christopher Langman as the heroic core of the narrative as the raft was constructed. When the raft was ready, Langman's contribution was to advise caution because of the lateness of the hour, a piece of advice that would prove correct when news of the Swede's death reached the survivors after their rescue.

The onset of starvation, John Deane's search for mussels and the death of the carpenter were all relayed in the pages of Jasper Deane's narrative. John Deane was the first to move the body. He was the chairman of the moral summit as to whether or not to eat the body. He was the one to skin the corpse when the crew refused. He was always leading by example even as his health deteriorated and his resolve was tested on a daily basis. In their initial refusal to eat human flesh, Christopher Langman and his two companions were portrayed in a more favourable moral light than even John or Jasper Deane.

As the narrative neared its conclusion the effects of cannibalism took their toll on the crew who degenerated into a form of barbarism. But John Deane remained disciplined in his eating, his rationing of flesh and his piety. In the Jasper Deane account, eating human flesh did not seem to have the same effect on John Deane as it did on the rest of the crew.

The rescue unfolded with John Deane concealing cannibalism from his deliverers. After a few false dawns the men were finally transported to New England, their last meal on Boon Island being broiled human flesh. The crew of the *Nottingham Galley* convalesced under the care of the New Englanders. Once they were well the survivors went their separate ways. John Deane, Christopher Langman 'and two or three more' returned to England.

Jasper Deane presented his version of the events with a vivid clarity. He had portrayed his brother as a heroic figure, privately vulnerable; a man who secretly agonised over difficult decisions but carried them out regardless, framing everything he did in the context of God's grace and sovereignty.

During the length of the narrative, Jasper Deane had been conspicuous in his restraint with regard to Christopher Langman, making no mention of the first mate's grievances. Jasper Deane was saving all his venom for the postscript. At the conclusion of the document Jasper Deane finally addressed the charges made against him, his brother and Charles Whitworth. Jasper Deane admitted that he had considered not dignifying Langman's accusations with a response but felt compelled to for the sake of 'truth and reputation'. Jasper Deane began his formal defence by tackling the privateer incident. He claimed that John Deane did not know about the insurance. He attested that John Deane would sooner empty his ship of crew and valuables, run her aground and then set her on fire than lose her to the French. Jasper Deane turned his attention to Langman's accusations that his brother deliberately shipwrecked the *Nottingham Galley* for insurance purposes: 'One would wonder malice itself could invent or suggest anything so ridiculous … that considers the extreme hazards and difficulties suffered by the commander himself, as well as his men, where 'twas more than ten thousand to one, but every man had perished … .'

Jasper Deane stated that the insurance gained on such a venture would amount to £226 7s. Deliberately wrecking a ship and risking the death of everyone involved would not be worth the risk. Christopher Langman's accusations made no sense. If there was any substance to the accusations of fraud, Jasper Deane demanded that his enemies prove it.

Christopher Langman's account of the Boon Island disaster was published toward the close of 1711. It was entitled: *A true account of the voyage of the Nottingham-Galley of London, John Deane Commander, from the River Thames to New-England.*

There was no circumspection in Langman's account. He began as he meant to go on with a sustained, angry assault on John Deane's character. In his brief introduction he set out his stall. He stated that the reason the *Nottingham Galley* had been wrecked was the 'captain's obstinacy'. He accused John Deane of trying to betray the vessel to the French. Langman stated that the agenda of his version of events was to expose 'the falsehoods in the captain's narrative'.

In the preface to Langman's account, the first mate's verdict on his former captain was that John Deane had treated his crew 'barbarously both by land and sea'. He accused John and Jasper Deane of rushing back to London to get their erroneous version of events into print before the truth could out. Langman made reference to Jasper Deane quoting those in England and New England that would attest to the veracity of the captain's version. Langman reminded Deane and informed the public that he had been ill and held to ransom in New England, that he was obliged to confirm John Deane's version of events for fear of being tipped out into the streets. Langman claimed that any dissenters to Deane's version of events were 'confined from appearing in public during our sickness,' and 'compelled to sign what our illness made us uncapable of understanding'. As soon as Langman and his companions were well they 'made out affidavits here sub-joined before Mr Penhallow, a Justice of the Peace, and a member of council at Portsmouth, New Hampshire, New England'. This was done in the presence of John Deane, 'who had not the face to deny it, his character appeared in a new light, and he was covered with shame and confusion'.

Christopher Langman addressed John and Jasper Deane's defence against the accusations of insurance fraud he had brought against them. Langman stated: 'we know nothing further of this matter than what we heard on board … *That there were great sums insured upon the ship,* the truth of which is more proper for the inquiry of others than us who are only sailors.' Langman pointed to the fact that he and two others had signed affidavits against Deane and company. Langman had done this under oath. He invoked the sanctity of that oath in the closing paragraph of his introduction:

And since what we deliver is upon oath, we hope it will obtain credit sooner than the bare word of Captain Deane, his brother and Mr Whitworth, who were all three interested persons, and but one of them, acquainted with all the matter of fact, which for his own reputation and safety he has been obliged to set in false colours. Besides, Mr Whitworth is since dead, so that the captain has no vouchers but himself and his brother; and how little credit they deserve, will sufficiently appear by what follows.

What followed was a narrative that gave full attention to the incident at Killybegs, overheard conversations about fraud and Deane's brutal treatment of his crew, culminating in the attempted murder of Christopher Langman hours before the *Nottingham Galley* was smashed to pieces on the rocks of Boon Island. The Captain John Deane of Langman's narrative was entirely without any redeeming features. When in control of the *Nottingham Galley* he was a violent tyrant. When catastrophe struck he was a gibbering coward. Langman's Deane was a lazy incompetent whose judgment was constantly being called into question by the more capable first mate. At any and every point during Christopher Langman's narrative John Deane's faults were highlighted, as were the points in the Jasper Deane narrative where the brothers had lied to make themselves look better. As Langman relayed the early stages of the sinking of the *Nottingham Galley*, he felt compelled to point out that John Deane had not rallied the crew to pray, nor had he ordered a terrified crew back on deck or ordered the cutting down of the mast. Langman praised the crew stating that they had not wilted 'under racks of conscience' as the Deane account had said they did. Deane had lied when he said that he had organised the advance party of swimmers to go ashore. He had lied about nearly drowning and losing his finger nails. Nobody swam ashore. The water had only been waist deep.

Once on Boon Island the broad facts of Langman's narrative largely aligned with those of the Jasper Deane account, punctuated with digs at John Deane. The men made a tent. The cook froze to death but John Deane did not 'show compassion' to the cook. The crew grew cold and hungry. The crew built a boat. The boat was smashed to pieces. Deane claimed the boat had a sail. Langman insisted there was no sail. The crew searched for food. John Deane stated that he wished he could have sold the cables and anchors and cannons of the *Nottingham Galley* for the men's subsistence, one the few human qualities attributed to John Deane by Christopher Langman. Langman killed his seagull. The raft was built. And although there seemed to be confusion over whether the heroic architect of the raft was Dutch or Swedish, it seemed to be a rare point of disagreement between Deane and Langman where there was no animosity. The carpenter died. John Deane rationalised that the cannibalisation of the carpenter was right and proper, with the implication that God had killed the carpenter so it was perfectly fine to eat him. Deane wanted to butcher the carpenter. Langman, George White and the boatswain abstained from cannibalism but gave in to their hunger the following day.

There was a break in the narrative for another inventory of accusations against John Deane. The captain was not welcome in the raft. John Deane did not look for provisions on his own. The dead carpenter's severed head and hands were not put in the ocean but left on the island. John Deane ate more human flesh than anybody else. The crew did not become animalistic after they had eaten human flesh. John Deane, Jasper Deane and Charles Whitworth did.

The crew were rescued.

Christopher Langman listed the survivors. Survival was credited to God's providence. In concluding his account, Langman launched a final salvo at his hated enemy. John Deane was a liar when he said that he spotted the sloop that facilitated their rescue. Deane exaggerated the danger he was in when he fell out of the canoe. When in New England John Deane's friend evicted him from his lodging when the captain terrorised his daughter. John Deane hogged the best of the relief for himself and had his own shipmates 'turned out of lodgings' before they were fully recovered.

Langman attested to the truth of his account. He ascribed that his motive for writing was, 'to testify our thankfulness to God for his great deliverance, and to give others warning not to trust their lives or estates in the hands of so wicked and brutish a man'. Finally Langman included copies of the three affidavits in his narrative to support his claim.

By the end of 1711 the two accounts of the shipwreck were in circulation and at war with one another. But other less credible versions were about to muddy the waters. A third account of the shipwreck was published by a J. Dutton. It appeared to be an unsolicited account drawing heavily on the Jasper Deane version. It contained a completely spurious reference to the crew of the *Nottingham Galley* eating 'bodies' as opposed to the singular carcass they actually consumed. There were mentions of the crew drawing lots to determine who would sacrifice themselves once the store of dead meat had been exhausted. In New England, a more credible version of the narrative was in circulation. The New England edition was in essence a truncated version of the Jasper Deane narrative. It was notable for the addition of a sermon about the Boon Island adventure by the Puritan preacher and pamphleteer Cotton Mather.

History would ultimately favour John and Jasper Deane's version of events. There were two obvious reasons for this. Christopher Langman died soon after the publication of his account and the vitality of his account died with him. In the absence of effective opposition John Deane was free to shape his own Boon Island narrative unopposed and as he saw fit. Throughout his life, John Deane would revisit the narrative and in a series of revisions and amendments offer back to the reading public the Boon Island story the way he wanted it to be remembered. But even if Langman had survived and dogged John Deane throughout his life with his own contrary versions of the Boon Island adventure, it was unlikely the public would have sided with him. John Deane's subsequent adventures would disprove many of Christopher Langman's accusations regarding his competence and character. But there were sections of his own narrative where Langman let himself down. Langman wanted to have it both ways. He was happy to accuse Deane and company of fraud and risk ruining the captain's reputation. He was perfectly articulate when making his case against the captain. But when the logic of Langman's accusations were called into question, specifically with respect to the practical illogic of John Deane's attempts at fraud, then Langman fell back on his own apparent lack of education, 'the truth of which is more proper for the inquiry of others than us who are only sailors'. According to Langman, such complicated notions were too lofty for a lowly sailor to contemplate. Langman had done his duty in reporting the accusation. The rest was for others to decode and decipher. But the worst blunder Langman made was overstating his case with regard to John Deane's villainy. John and Jasper Deane, whether by shrewd design or integrity, had been fair to Langman when they believed he merited it. They had attributed courage, industry and integrity to their former first mate, especially in regard to being among the last of the crew to give in to their hunger and eat human flesh. By contrast, Langman presented John Deane as such a drooling maniac as to push his version of the captain towards parody. In awarding little or no concession to John Deane's humanity, Langman was in danger of protesting too much and far too loudly.

In Langman's favour there was one great unanswered question. If John Deane was the injured party and there was no fraud or assault, then why did at least three members of his crew hate him so much that they sought to destroy his life by obliterating his reputation? No satisfactory answer survives. But history proved one thing about John Deane. He had a talent for making enemies; impassioned adversaries who despised him with deep and renewable reserves of hatred that Christopher Langman would have recognised and approved of.

The purpose of the original narratives had been to refute or prosecute accusations of fraud. But the efforts proved counterproductive. Whatever the public thought about Deane's innocence, the unifying image in their mind of the captain of the *Nottingham Galley* was that of an emaciated castaway who had eaten human flesh. England had become a place of poison and torment for John Deane. He felt the pressing need to leave his homeland and resculpt himself on some foreign shore and unfamiliar landscape.

Part Two

Soldier

Peter Alekseevich

In 1697 an unusually tall Russian gentleman was employed at the Royal Dockyards in Greenwich as a carpenter. The tall man was an avaricious student, soaking up and ingesting any and every piece of knowledge he could acquire about ship construction. The Russian was clearly an aristocrat affecting a position below his station for some unannounced purpose, spending time among the rough and the skilful of Deptford, absorbing their trade. The Russian was a strange and contradictory figure. He had come to London with something of an entourage but had stayed in a tiny house overlooking the Thames. He seemed to want to be treated with a level of informality but often acted with a bizarre degree of entitlement. His adventures became the talk of London. He slept with a famous actress. He had his portrait painted by Godfrey Kneller. He claimed to some that he was a merchant seaman or else a Russian officer but sought and received an audience with the Archbishop of Canterbury. He went by the name of Peter Mikhailov. He was in fact Peter Alekseevich, Peter the Great, the tsar of Russia, travelling incognito throughout Western Europe studying its culture and maritime knowledge. It was the worst kept secret on the continent.

The young tsar had already spent time in Sweden and the Dutch Republic. He had worked in the shipyards of the Dutch East India Company. He had studied under the master shipbuilder Class Paul. He had met with William of Orange. The Dutch welcomed him. They played the same game the English would play of knowing precisely who he was but pretending that they didn't know until it was obvious that he wanted them to know; then they would formally acknowledge his royal presence and accommodate him. Occasionally the tsar's anonymity would be taken at face value to his detriment. When in Riga, Peter the Great offended the Swedes when he paid a suspicious amount of attention to their ships and tried to sketch their fortifications. He was escorted from the harbour under armed guard. Whether the authorities were genuinely unaware of the tsar's identity or feigned ignorance in order to clip his wings is not certain. It was an error that they later would pay for in blood. But such confrontations were the exception during Peter the Great's tour of Europe. The tsar was accommodated. He was entertained and indulged. Generally speaking, his hosts were charmed and intrigued by him. They were also somewhat patronising and condescending regarding him. Peter Alekseevich could call himself what he wanted, see whatever and whomever he liked and study what he pleased. It made no difference. He might dress like a Western European and assimilate its wisdom but wasn't he just another gift-wrapped barbarian whose reach exceeded his grasp? It was a colossal misjudgement. Peter the Great returned to Russia with a harvest of maritime knowledge, experience and equipment. The English even gave him a ship, the *Royal Transport*, one of the best in Europe. During his tour the tsar would also visit Germany, Austria, Poland and Italy. He would utilise every scrap of information acquired. He would spend money and blood resculpting his vast land-hemmed nation into a formidable naval power. And every kingdom and administration that had given him assistance, even those that would technically consider him an ally, would regret the indulgence that they had once shown him.

Peter Alekseevich was 9 years old when he was crowned Peter I in 1682. The first decade or so of the young tsar's reign was a compromise necessitated by the factions that sought to control the gigantic country. Peter was forced to rule in name only alongside his feeble half-brother Ivan under the governance of his indifferent half-sister Sophia, who was content to cede all her authority to her lover. It was a violent and divided season, but by the time Peter was 22 years old he had wrested power back from his sister and had had her exiled.

The young Peter the Great was a progressive; openly contemptuous of ossified institutions. He was wild and hedonistic. He was arguably agoraphobic. He had a love of the grotesque; dwarves were part of his entourage and he was obsessed with deformed curiosities.

He was arrogant, yet there was a humility of industry about him. It was important to the tsar that he mastered any task he might order a subordinate to do. He was a man completely at odds with the heritage bequeathed him. The Russia of the late seventeenth century was a superstitious, backward and feudal nation. In the minds of most Western Europeans, Russia had barely trotted out of the Middle Ages. Peter the Great was an avid student of European ideas, architecture, fashion and warfare. He was determined to modernise Russia, use his formidable character to drag it, wailing if necessary, into a new era and command the attention and respect of the nations he had worshipped from afar. He forcibly reformed many of Russia's great institutions. He changed the Russian calendar to make it consistent with that of Western Europe. He banned the wearing of beards; on the surface a flippant reform but one that struck at the heart of the church where facial hair took on a totemic significance. He sent the sons of aristocrats to Western Europe to be educated. But Peter the Great understood that, for Russia to make any impression on the world stage, it was essential that it establish a credible and powerful naval presence in the Baltic. Without a navy, trade would be impossible. Sweden controlled the Baltic and, by extension, trade in that part of Europe. Sweden needed to be dealt with.

Before it could tackle Sweden on the water, Russia had to establish a defensible port. Russia, for all its size, was obstructed by its neighbours from creating any coastal foothold from which it might launch any prospective naval endeavour. Access to the Black Sea and the Caucasus was controlled by the Turks who occupied territory essential to Peter the Great's naval designs. In 1694 Peter the Great went to war with Turkey. The tsar's objective was to take the citadel of Azov on the River Don. Peter the Great laid siege to the citadel. He was defeated. The crucial ingredient in Russia's failure was their inability to stop the Turks resupplying Azov by water. In 1696 Peter the Great ordered a galley fleet to be constructed. It was a crude and basic flotilla but the fleet managed to stop Turkish resupply, allowing Peter the Great to besiege Azov for a second time without fear of relief. Azov fell. The tsar now had a scrap of land and a stretch of water from which he could start to build a better navy. A year after the fall of Azov, Peter began his tour of Europe.

On 30 July 1700 Russia signed a peace treaty with Turkey. One of the conditions of peace was that Russia retained Azov. Less than a month after securing peace with Turkey, Peter the Great declared war on Sweden.

The tsar did not believe in easing his people into change gradually. There was a new war with a formidable enemy, masters of an element alien to Russia. Building work began on the new capital of St Petersburg, an act of wilfulness that had a maritime logic to it but made little practical sense. The site of the new capital was marshland but situated on the River Neva. The Neva gave Russia entrance to the Gulf of Finland and by extension the rest of Europe. The tsar's great building project should not have worked but St Petersburg rose, stone by stone, from the swamp, built on the corpses of conscript labour, seemingly forced into existence by a tsar's will. Peter the Great would apply the same determination to building his navy.

The pretext for war with Sweden was tenuous to say the least. Peter the Great elected to take offence at the Swedes for escorting him from Riga under armed guard. War would be reparation for slighted honour. A second reason mooted for war was the reclamation of land that Sweden had taken between 1598 and 1613, an age of internal anarchy exploited by Russia's neighbours, known as the Time of Troubles. Peter the Great believed that he had timed his war perfectly. Sweden's king, Charles XII, was a youth and there were rumours of internal divisions. The War of Spanish Succession meant that the major powers of Western Europe were unlikely to interfere in a Baltic contest of arms. But the war went disastrously for Russia in its early stages. Peter the Great had formed a coalition with Poland and Denmark. The alliance collapsed. With a force of 40,000, Peter tried to take Narva, a Swedish-held port that would have given the tsar entry to the Baltic. The Russians were humiliated by a numerically inferior force. Around 8,000 of the tsar's soldiers were killed and 150 Russian guns were captured. Narva remained in Swedish hands. Sweden invaded Russia. The armies of Charles XII intended to march on Moscow. Russia's twin saving graces were its brutal weather, which destroyed supply lines and killed Russians and Swedes alike, and the immense Russian population from which Peter the Great could replace the dead lost at Narva and those killed by the elements. It bought the tsar enough time to regalvanise his forces and rethink his strategy. The tsar delivered a hammer blow to the Swedes at Polatva. It was a great victory but the tsar needed to duplicate his success on water for the war against the Swedes to mean anything at all. The naval victory Peter the Great was looking for arrived in 1714 at Hango Head.

The Battle of Hango Head took place near the Cape of Hango in Finland. The battle was a galley action. Swedish ships were tricked into shallow waters where they could not manoeuvre. Flat-bottomed Russian galleys hemmed the Swedes in. Peter the Great's forces boarded the Swedish vessels and took the ships plank by bloody plank in a gruelling bout of hand-to-hand fighting. Although gun-powder was expended, Hango Head was about as primitive a sea victory as Russia could have won, the methods of combat not dis-similar from those employed in the ancient battle of Salamis between the Persians and the Greeks. The Russians lost more men than the Swede's as they secured their victory but Hango Head was an arterial wound for Sweden. The Swedes lost two sloops, a frigate and half a dozen galleys, all taken as prizes by the Russians. The greater humili-ation was the capture of Rear Admiral Nilsson Ehrenskiold. Peter the Great would boast that not even the generals prosecuting the war against Louis XIV had taken such a prestigious prisoner. The tsar sent news to St Petersburg to prepare a triumph for the new fleet's return. Peter the Great returned home from battle and promoted himself to vice admiral of the Russian Fleet.

When he undertook the task of building a navy, Peter the Great was trying to create something out of nothing, a thing that had no precedent in Russian history. Russians did not know the sea or care to understand it. Foreign help was essential to any Russian success in the Baltic. And although nobody would ever credit the tsar with authentic humility, he was pragmatic enough to know that he needed to import expertise if he was ever to accomplish his great design. Aside from gathering experience and information, Peter the Great's trip to Europe had also been something of a headhunting expedition. The tsar was searching for talent, harvesting the best maritime hands and minds he could persuade to join him in Russia for his great adventure. The call had been put out. Skilled foreigners were welcome in Russia. And among the many foreigners that would serve in Peter the Great's navy was a haunted shipwreck cannibal trying to escape his past.

6

Babel

*J*ohn Deane had been invited to serve in the Russian navy. He had taken the offer to distance himself from the stigma of Boon Island. There was no real monetary incentive for him to serve but he stayed in Russia for nearly a decade. Few foreigners that served in Peter the Great's navy continued to serve for financial reward. Although the prospect of money might have attracted them in the first place, it became evident after a while that the pay was appalling compared to that offered in the navies of Western Europe. Soldiers of fortune stayed with Peter the Great largely because they had nowhere else better to go. The mercenaries so vital to the tsar's success were mainly exiles of one sort or another. John Deane carried the cross of scandal, but among the other human flotsam that washed up on Russia's shore were: John Perry, a one-armed sailor who had suffered court martial in England after the loss of a fire ship; Charles Van Werdan, a Swede who had turned against his own people; the brutal Italian Count de Buss; the drunkard Captain Black; the Norwegian privateer Vice Admiral Cruys; the incompetent Captain Little, who would later taint John Deane with the scent of his own scandal; and Peter Lacey, whom Deane would denounce in print as 'an Irish papist' who 'perpetrated innumerable devastations'. John Deane was a stigmatised English patriot who would find himself serving with many of his nation's natural enemies – the Dutch, the Irish and innumerable Jacobite Englishmen hounded out of their own country after the fall of James II.

Peter the Great had fashioned a utopia for the gifted and dispossessed of Western Europe. As far as the tsar was concerned, he had delivered a long overdue rebuke to Russia for its poor treatment of foreigners. Prior to Peter the Great's reforms, foreigners that had been resident in Russia's former capital had been forced to live apart in an area just outside of Moscow called the German Suburb. Now they were welcome in St Petersburg, their status – at least on the surface – radically elevated. But the reality was that Peter the Great had inadvertently created something of a snake pit. His foreigners would mistrust and turn on one another with regularity, and bloody consequences. The lion's share of Russians serving in Peter the Great's navy, who were in theory supposed to learn from their foreign teachers and replicate their knowledge, were envious and contemptuous of their tutors. Many careers and lives would be broken on the wheel of petty grievance and old tribal enmities. Yet somehow the navy worked, so long as Peter the Great was its beating heart, and for a long season John Deane would prosper as he served among its ranks.

John Deane had entered service in the Russian navy by 1714, the year of Hango Head. After the battle, the fortunes of foreign mercenaries were briefly favourable. Lieutenant Dunlop, an Irishman, was personally awarded 100 roubles by Peter the Great for volunteering to transport the tsar from ship to shore during a hard gale. Vice Admiral Cruys, who had been subject to a court martial the previous year, was recalled from exile in Kazan and made vice president of the College of Admiralty. Three Swedish vessels crewed by privateers were captured. Three ships arrived from England. But a 60-gun Russian warship exploded when it was struck by lightning during transportation across land. Unlike many of the tsar's foreigners, John Deane did not fight at Hango Head.

When the apocalyptic Russian winter fell, the rivers would freeze, the new harbours would become unnavigable and campaigning would cease until the spring thaw. This was a time to repair ships, drill crew and experiment with innovations. It was also a time to tacitly admit error and remove failing technology. In early 1714 poorly-designed boarding bridges that had been attached to Russian warships were taken away. In February the boarding bridges were sent to the port of Archangel by sledge. John Deane had not fought at Hango Head because he was part of the retinue sent to Archangel. Among the others were a mixture of under officers, lieutenants and seamen. Waiting for them at Archangel were four newly constructed ships: the *Uriel*, the *Salafiel*, the *Varakiel* and the *Egudal*. John Deane was given command of the *Egudal*.

Deane spent most of 1715 in Archangel. Elsewhere the war could be measured in raids, skirmishes and building plans. The Swedes shelled Revel Bay. The Russians responded in kind. There was something of a manpower shortage among the Russians and ships lay in haven for the absence of competent sailors. Peter the Great made preparations to turn Rager-Wik into a haven. The Russians encountered an English and Dutch squadron under the command of Sir John Norris, a great friend to the Russians but not necessarily a military ally. Civilities were exchanged. The controversial Count de Buss, who had committed atrocities on Dutch flyboats carrying neutral flags, died and was replaced as rear admiral of the galleys by Captain Commodore Ismaivitz.

In September 1715 John Deane was ordered to sail the Egudal from Archangel to the Baltic. The captains of the Salafiel, the Varakiel and the Uriel would do the same. Accompanying them was a transport yacht given as a present to the tsar by William of Orange.

John Deane suffered an immediate setback. The *Egudal* sprang a leak. Deane was forced to return. The *Uriel*, the *Salafiel* and the *Varakiel* reached the safety of Norway and Copenhagen and wintered there. The royal yacht fared badly. Near the Swedish coast the yacht was cast away and lost. The *Egudal* was repaired and made seaworthy. John Deane set sail later than he would have liked. He set sail later than was reasonably safe to do so. Harsher than any New England winter, the Baltic elements were murderous at this time of year and Deane would pay the penalty in frozen flesh. As he sailed on, the furies of Boon Island raked his boat as the ice and the wind slaughtered his crew one by one. By the time he had delivered his vessel, half of his men were dead. But Deane was alive. For the second time he had proved that the cold could not kill him. His ship was intact. There would be no censure. He had obeyed orders under difficult conditions. This was Russia. The loss of life was just one of those things. Winter kills. John Deane had done nothing wrong. He would be allowed to progress.

Half of John Deane's crew froze to death transporting a Russian warship from Archangel to the Baltic. *Illustration by Stephen Dennis*

The year 1716 began as the years always did, with promotions. But the initial military objective of the New Year was to coordinate the army and the navy. Part of the fleet was stationed at Revel. Under the command of the Dutchman Captain Commodore Sievers, as soon as the weather allowed, the Revel squadron was to meet up with the rest of the fleet and their Danish allies and sail to Copenhagen. The Russians and the Danish intended to advance together through Scania but the squadron discovered that the Swedish fleet was waiting near Copenhagen. Sievers and company returned to Revel. The Russian fleet that had been sailing in the North Sea gathered at Flekkero, Norway. John Deane sailed into Flekkero in April. Sievers arrived in May. Deane set sail for Copenhagen with the squadron on 27 May.

Two days later the squadron met the British fleet, commanded by Sir John Norris. The combined force sailed to Copenhagen.

Rifts and fatal breaches of etiquette were rife in the Russian navy at this time. There was a mutiny about pay among seamen and under officers; eighty men deserted and fled to Holland. A Dutchman, Captain Black, saluted Sir John Norris by striking his pendent at the same time that the Englishman struck his own pendent. From a Russian perspective this was considered highly insulting to their English ally. In Holland it was not considered insulting at all. In Russia the insult carried the death sentence. The situation was further complicated by the fact that Captain Black was drunk when he committed his faux pas. Black was subject to a court martial. He escaped capital punishment but was confined at Revel where he drank himself to death.

The Dutch Captain Commodore Wybrant Scheltinga tried to tackle the partisanship that divided the fleet. Factions fell in behind two captains, the Norwegian Peter Bredale and the Russian Ivan Sinavin. John Deane favoured Bredale. Deane despised Sinavin calling him, 'a sordid, drunken, ignorant fellow, a creature of the tsar's, and therefore of great power misused by him, to the exposing of himself and his Prince's service to ridicule.' Deane's assessment of Sinavin's worth as a human being and an officer was typical of the escalating contempt in which he would come to hold most of the Russians he encountered and of the ambivalent attitude he felt towards the tsar that governed them.

On 7 July, Peter the Great arrived in person bringing with him thirty-seven galleys and a snow. On 20 July he took command as vice admiral. Since the battle of Polatva, the creaky alliance with Denmark had been somewhat refortified. Peter the Great entertained the king of Denmark and set his mind to reorganising the fleet. The tsar initiated something of a reshuffle among his officers. He was concerned about the polyglot nature of his fleet. He reassigned officers to ships best suited to their abilities. Once assigned, the captains would stay with the same ship, an antidote to the problems of negotiating the different languages and maritime cultures that made up the body of the fleet. He insisted that any commanders must have risen the ranks and be skilled navigators familiar with the coasts. The *Egudal* was taken from John Deane and he was given a new vessel, a frigate. John Deane was now captain of the *Samson*.

The *Samson* was built in Holland. It was a gift to Peter the Great from the tsar's close companion Prince Alexander Danivolovich Menishikoff. It was a relatively small vessel, bristling with guns. There were forty of them. But forty was considered too many guns for the size of vessel. The English master builder Richard Brown overhauled the *Samson* and reduced the guns to a more manageable thirty-two. Deane's assessment of Brown's handiwork was that he had turned the *Samson* into 'an excellent frigate'. Prior to Hango Head the *Samson* had been employed to look for the Swedish fleet, avoid a confrontation and alert the Russians of their enemy's whereabouts. After Hango Head the *Samson* hunted privateers, capturing three enemy vessels. The *Samson* was sent on missions to England and Holland. The *Samson* was fitted with, and then stripped of, the contentious boarding equipment John Deane would help transport across Russia by sledge. Prior to Deane, the *Samson* had been commanded by another Englishman, Benjamin Edwards, and two Norwegians, Isaac Brandt and Peter Bredale. Under the new administration John Deane would stay with the *Samson* until promotion, death, demotion or disgrace separated him from her.

When Peter the Great assumed command of the fleet, John Deane got the opportunity to test the guns of his new vessel when a salute was fired in honour of the tsar. Once the tsar's fleet had been reorganised it was ready to find the Swedes and force a confrontation if the conditions favoured the Russians. But John Deane's orders were to wait upon Sir John Norris and find out if he had any intentions of committing his cruisers to the ensuing conflict. If the answer was 'yes' then Deane and fellow Englishman William Baker would accompany the English cruisers, Deane in the *Samson* and Baker in the *Arundel*. Sir John Norris declined to commit his ships so the tsar ordered Deane and Baker to search for the Swedish fleet and report back the Swedes' strength and numbers.

and of gunfire. Sir John Norris had
enty-one-gun salute. The tsar recipro-
ships fired their own friendly salvos.

e Russian fleet set sail for the Danish island of
is's squadron, a number of merchant vessels and
-of-war accompanied them. John Deane located the
eet. They had sailed to the naval port of Karlskrona. Deane
ret ed to the Russians and reported the news.

A proposed plan to invade Sweden came to nothing. The campaigning season juddered to a halt as winter approached. John Deane's last mission of 1716 was to patrol the Baltic in the *Samson* alongside Captain Baker in the *Arundel*. Deane and Baker's orders were to 'keep different courses in the Baltic,' in order to find and harry enemy store ships that were believed to be in the vicinity.

7

Apraxin

s 1716 drew to a close, a few of the tsar's ships were lost to the elements; a four-gun privateer was captured and there was a controversy involving a Dutch officer. Captain Vandergun had sold items aboard Deane's previous vessel, the *Egudal*. The items were not his to sell, an act tantamount to theft. His peers informed on him. Vandergun was arrested. He was subject to court martial and was sentenced to three years' confinement. On closer investigation it transpired that Vandergun had had no money to feed his men and had only sold the items to buy food for that purpose. Deane was convinced that those that had told tales about Vandergun's justifiable indiscretion had been motivated by covetousness, craving the Dutchman's command.

The fleet wintered at Revel. A storm destroyed part of Revel and broke two ships to pieces, the *Fortune* and the *Antonio*. The tsar was in St Petersburg. In his absence there were few promotions. No important decisions were allowed to be made in his absence so nothing much was accomplished until he returned.

On 12 April 1717, the day the ice broke, John Deane set sail with new orders. He was to briefly visit his homeland. Deane transported apprentices bound for five years' service to Rostock, England and then Holland. By July, he had returned, and John Deane and the *Samson* were placed in a squadron under the command of General Admiral Fedor Matveevich Apraxin.

The general admiral was one of the few Russians John Deane had a kind word to say about. Deane's physical description of him was a man 'well made' and 'inclined to feed', a polite or mischievous euphemism for fat. Apraxin had long white hair that he tied in a

General Admiral Fedor Matveevich Apraxin, John Deane's first great mentor. Apraxin's patronage secured John Deane safe passage out of Russia after the English captain's court martial. *Illustration by Jean Nightingale*

ribbon. He was in his mid-fifties. He was a childless widower. He was neat and dressed, in Deane's opinion, in a manner that 'surpasses all the noblemen of his years in Russia'. Apraxin was an even-tempered individual. He liked men to behave according to their rank and station, and expected to be treated with the deference due his own rank. He didn't suffer fools. He was a man of his word. He did not extend patronage easily but when he did he was fiercely protective of his charges. Where Apraxin was concerned, Deane abandoned his stance of denigrating Russians with little or no naval experience. Deane respected the on-the-job knowledge Apraxin had accrued. Deane's assessment of Apraxin's relationship with the tsar was that the Admiral was more 'esteemed than loved' by Peter the Great, 'and therefore rarely consulted, unless on arduous and important affairs'. On this point Deane was in error. Apraxin was a close friend and intimate confidant of the tsar. There was also a shadow side to the admiral. He could be a rough and brutal man when he believed necessity demanded it. In the aftermath of an early revolt, Apraxin had hanged rebels on the roads leading in and out of Voronezh. In 1718 the tsar's son Alexi Petrovich would rebel against his father. Apraxin would be present at his interrogation and torture. Alexi Petrovich would be brutally flogged and die later that day. But Apraxin showed the conciliatory and paternal part of his nature to many of Peter the Great's foreign mercenaries and it was the better part of Apraxin that John Deane encountered at close quarters. Deane would recall an incident between Captain Commodore Sievers and the English Jacobite exile Rear Admiral Thomas Gordon. Sievers and Gordon were celebrating the anniversary of the Battle of Hango Head. Both men were roaring drunk. Gordon insulted Sievers, claiming he had taken the best sailors for himself prior to Hango Head. When news reached the tsar of the dispute, Apraxin defended the Dutchman to his ruler and criticised Gordon. The tsar refused to take sides and forced the two enemies to have a conciliatory drink together. Despite Apraxin's intervention tensions continued to fester and engendered factions within the fleet. Gordon recruited a strong ally in Rear Admiral Thomas Saunders, a man that would cause John Deane particular grief in years to come. But Apraxin's example was not lost on Deane, who would have reason to thank the admiral when his own Russian adventure turned to ash.

The fleet anchored near Ostergarn. John Deane and Clays Eckoff, the Danish captain of the *Portsmouth*, were ordered to sail southward toward Slite Hamn where they were to observe enemy fortifications and report back on the enemy's strength.

The Russian fleet entered Ostergarn. They encountered a small amount of enemy resistance from mounted guns that the Swedes quickly spiked before retreating and lighting warning beacons. The Russian fleet anchored and put soldiers ashore.

Deane and Eckoff approached Slite Hamn. They sailed within shooting range of the fortifications. A gale was blowing. Deane and Eckhoff measured the depth of the water and observed the fortress. The fort was situated on an island that was, according to Deane, 'disunited from the mainland by the passage into the harbour'. Deane spotted batteries of guns camouflaged behind foliage. Deane and Eckhoff ordered their men to fire the cannons of the *Samson* and the *Portsmouth* at the batteries. The Swedes fired all their guns at once in retaliation. Deane and Eckhoff counted the guns. They had the information they needed. The *Samson* and the *Portsmouth* returned to the fleet.

At Ostergarn, cruisers were sent north and south to stand watch and send warning if the Swedish fleet were nearby. Two of the cruisers, the *Poltava* and the *Elias*, spotted a small privateer. They pursued her. The crew of the privateer could not outpace the cruisers so they took their vessel into shallow water where it would be difficult for the heavier cruisers to follow. The privateers ran their vessel aground. They stripped her of her guns and took them ashore. The *Poltava* and the *Elias* dispatched smaller boats to the privateers' vessel. What they were supposed to have done was to attach ropes to the abandoned vessel, drag her into deeper water and take her back to Ostergard. Instead they tried to set her on fire. The *Poltava* sailed back to the fleet. The *Elias* stayed behind to prevent the privateers, who were currently stranded on shore with their guns, from facilitating their escape by returning to the boat and putting out the fire. When the *Poltava* came back, her captain gave his report to General Admiral Apraxin.

John Deane was present when Captain Van Gent told General Admiral Apraxin what had happened. Apraxin listened in complete disbelief. Deane had come to see Apraxin to present a report on his findings at Slite Hamn. Apraxin rebuked the Dutch officer and then turned to Deane. Apraxin ordered Deane back onto the *Samson* and gave him free reign to take any ship or boat he needed. Apraxin ordered Deane to find the privateers' vessel and either retrieve or else utterly destroy her. Once either task had been accomplished, Deane was to go ashore with an armed contingent and take the guns from the Swedish privateers. Apraxin promised John Deane a generous reward if he could successfully carry out his new orders. Deane set sail with two longboats, a few pinnaces and enough armed men to retrieve the guns. It was John Deane's first real opportunity to distinguish himself in combat, advance himself and make some money. Deane's own allies let him down. When the *Samson* approached the *Elias*, the *Elias* was alone in the water. Somehow the captain and the crew of the *Elias* had allowed the privateers to reboard their vessel, put out the fire and escape, guns and all. John Deane, the *Samson* and the *Elias* sailed back to General-Admiral Apraxin empty-handed.

There was no censure for John Deane. He had done nothing wrong. But there would be charges to answer for the commanding officers of the *Elias* and the *Poltava* when the fleet docked at Revel.

The fleet engaged in a little light looting before they left for Revel. They took cattle from the surrounding countryside but refrained from destroying any property. When the fleet arrived in Revel a court martial was held for the officers of the *Elias* and the *Poltava*. Apraxin wanted to cashier the officers of both vessels. The members of the court martial were more lenient. The officers of the *Poltava* walked away without punishment. Captain Ducy of the *Elias* was dismissed from the service. His lieutenant was also disciplined. Apraxin went into the country for a short respite. He left the New Englander Rear Admiral George Paddon in charge with orders to engage the fleet in military exercises. Paddon made a pig's ear of carrying out his orders. The exercises were conducted with much disorder and tensions among the fleet were allowed to fester. There was some consolation in the capture of an enemy snow but even that gave way to disagreements about whether the Dutch captain of the *Pearl* or the Hanoverian captain of the *Alexander* had taken her. In August, Paddon left with eleven of the fleet's finest ships for the Russian port of Kronslot, where he intended to winter. The Russian fleet was strengthened by new ships from Copenhagen.

At some point during the campaigning season, John Deane pursued and captured two Swedish merchantmen in the Gulf of Danzig. Once a ship had been taken as a prize, the protocol was to man the captured vessel with capable members of your own crew, who would sail the vessel back to Revel. Deane was engaged in the process of selecting which of his men would crew the merchantmen when two warships were spotted. It was not a cause for immediate concern. One ship was a Dutch man-of-war and the other an English frigate. Both nations were allies to Russia. What happened next took John Deane completely by surprise. The frigate and the man-of-war demanded at gunpoint that Deane give up the merchantmen. It was a delicate moment that required a pragmatic response. The English and the Dutch were supposed to be compatriots. The *Samson* would be shot to pieces if Deane elected to fight them. Deane surrendered the merchantmen. The English and the Dutch let Deane go. Deane reported the incident to his superiors. Russian naval command, who would often be guilty of disregarding the context in which difficult decisions had to be made, seemed to understand why Deane had acted the way he did. There was no censure. Deane had done nothing wrong.

In September, Peter the Great returned to Revel where he inspected and approved of the building work that had been taking place there. He was approached by a delegation of English merchants. They had missed a convoy that would have provided them with the necessary protection through the volatile waters that constituted part of their trade route. The English appealed to the tsar for help. The tsar ordered the *Samson* and the *Uriel* to provide an escort. John Deane took the merchants to Danzig. When they tried to go further they were forced to turn back because of bad weather. Deane wintered at Revel. There was little else for him to do that year.

As 1717 drew to a close, three new ships from St Petersburg were added to the fleet, a new administrative naval rank of secretary was introduced and cabin boys made their first appearance in the Russian navy. There was extensive building work to link key ports with St Petersburg via a network of canals. There were expeditionary voyages to the Caspian Sea.

The next year began with the usual batch of promotions, including one for Captain Commodore Scheltinga who, despite being mortally ill and paralysed down one half of his body, was promoted to the rank of rear admiral of the red. The promotion was interpreted by Deane as a sop from Peter the Great to the stricken officer so that he would have 'the honour of dying a rear admiral'.

The fleet were instructed to be ready to sail as soon as the ice broke. Deane was given sealed orders and told to open them when he was 20 leagues from Revel. He set sail and broke the seal as instructed. Along with the Uriel and the Randolph, John Deane was ordered to, 'proceed and cruise at large on the enemy's coast, to hinder all trade with Sweden, and make prizes of all nations, French and Hollanders excepted'. Captain John Deane had been given a hunting licence. He had clear but flexible instructions and a degree of autonomy to pursue and board most ships he encountered. But the chances for financial remuneration were not as glittering as they first appeared. The new rank of secretary was designed to ensure that everything taken from a boarded ship was properly logged and accounted for. Every ship had to have a secretary. But despite this new added layer of bureaucracy, Deane must have felt optimistic. This was his best chance so far to forge a reputation in war that might expunge his sense of shame for deeds done in the name of survival on a scrap of rock off the New England coast.

8

Prizes

The man who had once been accused of deliberately trying to lose his vessel to privateers found, now that the tables had been turned, that he showed a real aptitude for the trade; for state-approved piracy was effectively his profession now. John Deane set sail in June 1718. He had only been at sea a month when the *Samson* and the *Pearl* returned to Revel with four Swedish vessels in tow. Two of the prizes may have been captured by Deane working in conjunction with the *Pearl*, or the *Pearl* may have captured them herself. But half the tally belonged to Deane. In fact John Deane had employed an outrageous degree of panache to snare his two captured vessels. Deane had disguised the *Samson* as a Swedish ship and sailed her right into Burgs Vic harbour in Gotland. He had joked and laughed with the gulled Swedes and then took two of their ships away from them. It was a cavalier beginning to a grand run that would total twenty-two prizes.

Once the initial quartet of prizes had been delivered, the *Samson* and the *Pearl* returned to the open sea to hunt for more. The prizes mounted up. In an echo of the incident that had cost him his reward the previous year, John Deane was afforded the opportunity to demonstrate the correct way of dealing with a stricken enemy trapped in shallow waters. Deane was in pursuit of a Swedish privateer. The privateer tried to evade the *Samson* by sailing into a creek where she knew the pursuing frigate was too big to follow. The Swedes had started to carry their guns ashore. Deane manoeuvred the *Samson* as close to the creek as was safe to do so without grounding his own ship. Then Deane ordered his men to fire the *Samson*'s cannons and force the Swedes away from their own guns. The Swedes succeeded in getting four guns off the boat, then decided to cut their losses. The Swedes torched their own ship. John Deane dispatched a pinnace. The men in the pinnace were ordered to board the burning Swedish vessel where they successfully retrieved the enemy's guns and ammunition.

While John Deane was chasing privateers, Peter the Great was pre-occupied with building a new haven at Rager-Wik. The plans came to nothing and he ordered a house built for himself instead. In August the *Samson* and the *Pearl* returned to Revel. They were quickly refitted and set out for the third time that year to hunt for enemy ships. The *Samson* and the *Pearl* rewarded the confidence placed in them and returned with more prizes.

The rest of the summer played out like some sort of farcical martial children's game as ships were taken and retaken by an array of different nations. The Swedes recaptured two ships the Russians had taken as prizes. One of those ships was retaken by the Russians. The Dutch and the English seized two of their own ships that the Russians had undiplomatically taken as prizes. There were further tensions between the Russians and the Dutch over the issue of saluting. Two Russian officers were imprisoned by the Governor of Pilau in retaliation against the Russians when they took two enemy ships within proximity of his castle. But two new ships were added to the Russian fleet, the *Lesnoy* and the *Hango Head*.

As winter settled and 1719 was ushered in, there was a slew of promotions among the high-ranking officers of the Russian fleet. Rear Admiral Paddon, who had made such a mess of Apraxin's orders to drill the Russian fleet, had died and was replaced by Prince Menishikoff. The feuding Captain Commodores Sievers and Gordon were promoted to rear admirals of the blue and red respectively. Admiralty College was now fully established. The new institution's responsibilities were to manage pay, victualling, issuing orders to flag officers and publicising the details of court martial. Men-of-war and galleys were made ready for the new campaigning season and midshipmen were introduced to the Russian navy for the first time.

The ice thawed. Deane and the *Samson* sailed out alongside the *Pearl*, the *Pink Alexander*, the *Elias* and the *Lansdowne*. The captains opened their orders. They were commanded to 'obstruct, as much as possible, all trade to and from Sweden by making prizes of all nations tracking thither without exception'. The transports were instructed to reach the Swedish shore near Karlskrona by nightfall. The cruisers were to stay hidden until dark and then rendezvous with the transports. A coordinated incursion into Swedish territory was to take place. The intention was to snatch 'what people of fashion should fall in their way, in order to get intelligence on the real state of the Swedish fleet,' and then, 'by an alarm given [...] facilitate the intended descent in a different quarter'. In other words, once the Swedish fleet's strength and position had been determined, the Russians would launch a land assault on Swedish territory, in an agreed location, where the Swedish navy was unlikely to be.

The cruisers approached the prearranged destination. There was a conference. Present at the conference was Count Nicholas Golovin, a protégé of Peter the Great. Although Golovin only held the rank of a lieutenant it was publicised that he would 'command the present descent'. The feeling among those who outranked him was that the tsar was creating an opportunity for the count to notch up a victory so that he might later be preferred with some degree of credibility. But the count was not so keen to grasp the nettle presented to him by his ruler and patron. He wanted to know whether there were enemy soldiers in the coastal villages before he led the descent. His reluctance delayed the mission.

John Deane received fresh orders. He was to set out in the *Samson* on a three-day intelligence-gathering mission. He returned with three prizes. He handed certain captured passengers over to be interrogated. It was hoped that the information gleaned might provide more clarity as to whether the proposed descent into Sweden was to take place. Nothing came of the interrogations. The descent was no nearer happening.

Deane and the *Samson* were dispatched for another three days. This time the *Lansdowne* sailed with the *Samson*. Deane was given command over both vessels. Deane's verdict on the *Lansdowne* was that she was 'an old and crazy' ship, 'altered from forty to twenty-four guns'. Deane's mission this time was to 'cruise near the river of Stockholm' in search of the post yacht that ferried mail from Stockholm to Visby. The 'river of Stockholm' was in reality a fjord. The fjord became Deane's hunting ground for seven rather than the three days ordered. In that brief space of time, John Deane was terrifying in his industry. He captured fourteen prizes and took an extremely valuable prisoner, Captain Monsieur Van Merch, privy councillor to the king of Prussia. Van Merch's currency as a captive rested in the fact that he had recently been present in Stockholm and was conversant with the state of things internally in the enemy country. The *Samson* and the *Lansdowne* sailed back to the fleet with a flotilla of prizes and their valuable captive. They were obstructed by a savage gale. The prizes were not up to sailing in such violent conditions. The *Samson* and the *Lansdowne* arguably were, but had spread their crews so thinly among the captured vessels that they had rendered themselves vulnerable to the hostile elements. Deane and his small fleet were forced to sail for the protection of Revel.

Deane delivered all fourteen prizes. He sent a courier to inform the tsar of Van Merch's capture. He handed Van Merch over to the commander of the *Lansdowne*. He ordered him to wait for the courier's return so that the tsar's will might be made known. Deane stayed in Revel for a couple of days before setting sail on 21 May. Van Merch was taken to Kronslot, interviewed and then released two days or so later.

In Deane's absence, two enemy ships and a snow had been captured. The fleet were starting to wonder where Deane was and sent ships to find him and the *Lansdowne*. More prizes were taken and a new ship, the *Isaac Victoria*, was launched. By 2 June, most of the cruisers had come back to Revel. Their orders were to stay put and wait for the fleet coming from Kronslot under the command of Peter the Great himself. But the Kronslot fleet was delayed when the *Lesnoy*, a ship that the tsar had personally helped to build, sank in the harbour when it struck an anchor that ripped a hole in its underbelly. The Kronslot fleet eventually arrived in Revel on 20 June. The fleet stayed in Revel for three days. Prizes were distributed and there were promotions.

On 23 June the fleet sailed from Revel. On 27 June they reached Hango Head. Deane and the *Samson* were sent to 'observe the motion' of the nearby British squadron commanded by Sir John Norris. While Deane was engaged in what was effectively a spying mission on his own countrymen, the fleet at Hango Head saw their tsar devolve his command of the fleet to Peter Sievers and then join the galley fleet. The fleet sailed a day later on 3 July. They were joined by two Danish frigates. Russia's various alliances were now riddled with mutual suspicion. Supposed friendly nations took one another's ships as prizes, Englishmen 'observed' Englishmen, and the two Danish frigates were thought to be spy ships. Paranoia infected the Russian fleet.

Peter the Great left the main fleet and took the galleys to Aland, a preparatory manoeuvre to ready the harbour of Rodham for the advent of the Russian fleet. The fleet assembled in Rodham. John Deane returned. Deane was removed from the *Samson* and given command of a sixty-gun man-of-war, the *Devonshire*, one of the finest ships in the fleet.

9

Court Martial

Peter the Great called a council of war. Both the navy and the army were present. Key ministers in Peter the Great's government were also there. There was discussion about the proposed descent into Swedish territory. According to Deane, such was the nature of the debate that, 'the tsar ordered his ministers, generals and flag officers to deliver in writing the next morning their sentiments concerning the intended descent'.

The following day the galley fleet, under the protection of half a dozen men-of-war, sent raiders from the galleys ashore. The raiders scoured the enemy country and returned with many civilian prisoners who were taken captive to St Petersburg. The tsar recalled the galley fleet on 18 August. Peter the Great left the main fleet on 21 August to return to Kronslot, taking the galleys with him. Before he left he spoke to his officers. The tsar was in a good mood and thanked his men for 'their good services'.

The main Russian fleet, now under the command of Admiral Sievers, sailed for Revel with many recently taken prizes. John Deane and the *Devonshire* sailed with the fleet, arriving at Revel on 24 August. The British fleet was expected. The immediate priority was to ascertain its whereabouts as quickly as possible. Near the Isle of Nargen, the Kronslot Squadron waited for Sir John Norris and the British. Cruisers went looking for them. Fire beacons sat ready to be ignited, to relay news in a chain of flame once the British had been discovered. The fleet readied itself for dual possibilities, either the advent of the British or else the appearance of the elusive Swedish navy.

On 22 September Adjutant General Alexander Ivanovitz Rumanzoff, the man who had hunted down the tsar's rebellious son

Alexei and brought him captive back to his father, arrived in Revel. He had orders from the tsar. Three of the best ships in the fleet were to sail to Kronslot as soon as they could make themselves ready. The *London*, the *Portsmouth* and the *Devonshire* were selected. Robert Little commanded the *London*, Adam Urquhart the *Portsmouth* and John Deane the *Devonshire*.

According to Deane, the next few days were spent in 'much hurry and confusion,' making the ships ready 'with all possible expedition'. The three ships set sail on 25 September. On 29 September the *London* and the *Portsmouth* were 5 leagues from Kronslot, ahead of Deane and the *Devonshire* by a distance of 2 miles. The *London* and the *Portsmouth* had plotted a different course from the one Deane had instructed his own men to follow. Both the *London* and the *Portsmouth* hit a sandbank. Both ships ran aground. Imprisoned by the shallows and the sand the *London* and the *Portsmouth* were at the mercy of Deane and any help and expertise he might provide.

John Deane weighed anchor. He sent a boat to Kronslot to seek out the commanding officer and ask for help. Kronslot sent boats to aid the *London* and the *Portsmouth*. Deane ordered Little and Urquart to be ferried to the *Devonshire* where the three Englishmen discussed how best to dislodge the two paralysed warships. The situation was difficult and embarrassing but not insurmountable. Then the weather turned.

The volatile elements obstructed any further help from Kronslot. Little and Urquhart returned to their ships and attempted to cut down their masts. In his spartan account of what followed, Deane did not reveal how, but during the felling of the *London*'s mast, Captain Urquhart was killed. The *London* and the *Portsmouth* were bilging. John Deane had sent many of his own men and every boat that he had to try and dislodge the ships from the sandbank. All of Deane's boats were destroyed or lost in the attempt. Deane had done everything he could. He had laboured for three days to help rescue the *Portsmouth* and the *London*. Now he needed to be pragmatic and secure the safety of his own vessel and such crew that were still aboard. On 1 October John Deane severed the *Devonshire*'s cable and sailed for Kronslot. Captain Little would be rescued eventually but the *Portsmouth* and the *London* would not be recovered. The aftermath of the Kronslot incident would be a toxic experience for both surviving commanding officers.

It was inevitable Captain Little would be called to account for the loss of the *London*. But there was a contingent in Kronslot that believed that John Deane was equally to blame. There was a perverse irony to the accusations against Deane. In an inversion of the charges of incompetence that Christopher Langman had once levelled at Deane, it would be his skill and experience that would be the rod by which his enemies sought to beat him this time. The logic supporting the case against Deane was that Little and Urquhart were vastly inexperienced in comparison. Deane was better acquainted with the coasts and should have schooled the less-experienced captains to circumvent the sandbanks that he had managed to avoid. There was a further implication to the accusation against Deane. Deane was thought by many to have purposefully allowed Captain Little to ground his ship by deliberately withholding crucial information about the sandbanks from him. The motive for such treachery was believed to have been the outworking of some feud between the two men. The Machiavellian logic ascribed to Deane was discounted when investigations revealed the fact that Little and Urquhart had sailed ahead of Deane, and that 2 miles and half an hour separated the *Devonshire* from the *London* and the *Portsmouth*. The inevitable court martial cleared Deane. Captain Little was demoted to lieutenant and sentenced to six months' confinement. The mate of the *London* was sent to the galleys. John Deane contemptuously ascribed Captain Little's blunder to, 'ignorance and too much pride to ask for advice'.

Deane did not succeed in walking away from the affair without something of a breach to his standing. He had survived the often unpredictable and inconsistent ordeal of a Russian court martial. But a grain of doubt had been planted in the mind of Peter the Great. When the ships ran aground the first scrap of news that reached the tsar had been that a single vessel had run into trouble. This news alone had brought the tsar to Kronslot. When he heard that a second ship had run aground his mood had darkened considerably. Peter the Great took the loss of any of his ships personally. The *London* and the *Portsmouth* were two of his best. The fact that Deane had preserved the *Devonshire* counted for very little in the tsar's eyes. Although John Deane had been technically exonerated, he was personally convinced that Peter the Great harboured suspicions about him. There were rumours circulating to the effect that the tsar privately believed the loss of his two beloved vessels was down to 'party emulation'. Whether this was true or not, the perception was in the ether that Deane was a partisan who prized tribal enmities above service to the tsar and who would sacrifice a ship to prosecute a grudge.

For a long uninterrupted season, John Deane had triumphed in the Russian navy. He had captured numerous prizes. He had won the confidence of Admiral Apraxin. He had proven himself an expert and flamboyant thief of foreign shipping. In Russia success bred enmity. With royal and aristocratic patronage Deane had become somewhat untouchable, but now the tsar had removed his hand, Deane's position had been weakened. It was evident that Deane had enemies. He had been assaulted. He had survived the assault but not without wounding. Blood was in the water and predators were being drawn to the scent.

The pretext for John Deane's second great fall was an incident that was two years old and for which he had received no censure at the time. There was a groundswell of resentment toward Deane for the favour that he had won. His enemies were Russians, officers who did not share their tsar's love of foreigners, who resented being tutored by them but nevertheless desired their rank and status. It was a question of timing. Deane's enemies exploited the current willingness to believe ill of the Englishman. Deane's loss of the two ships to the English and the Dutch in 1717 was now seen as grounds for court martial. Deane was dragged before a military tribunal for the second time that year. The charge was collusion with the enemy. Deane was accused of taking money from the English and the Dutch in exchange for the captured merchantmen. Deane called on a dozen or so officers from the *Samson* to testify that he had done no such thing. Unlike the divided loyalties of the crew of the *Nottingham Galley*, Deane's subordinates defended his reputation. Deane had one Russian ally. Admiral Apraxin did not interfere directly in the mechanics of the court martial but in a roundabout way Apraxin came to the aid of his protégé. He gave Deane a passport. The passport released Deane 'from service at his own request to return to his homeland'. But Deane was finished. The trial was a formality. Deane's fall was rapid. He was found guilty. His punishment was a year in prison. But there was a degree of mercy to leaven the judgment. Peter the Great himself commuted Deane's sentence from imprisonment to service in Kazan, presumably a concession to Deane for years of exemplary service up until the point of disgrace. But John Deane was stripped of his rank and demoted to lieutenant.

Peter the Great's act of mercy was double-edged. Deane's sentence was still severe. Kazan was 130 miles from Moscow. Kazan was the main source of timber for the Russian navy. Deane's punishment was to transport timber from Kazan to Lagoda Lake. The route was involved and perilous; a long and convoluted journey that took a transport vessel along the Volga and Tvertsa rivers, navigating shallow water near Vishni-Volochok, moving against the current. The transport vessel was at the mercy of the high water, travel in late summer being virtually impossible. The later stages of the journey were navigable by canal and a small river that granted the transport access to Lake June and then Lagoda Lake where the timber would be delivered and then taken to St Petersburg. Deane described the dangers of the later stage of the journey:

> The navigation on the lake is very difficult by reason of the deep water, few harbours, sorry shipping and the inexperience of the Russian seamen; and great is the danger of passing the three falls, in the entrance to the Neva. So that many vessels are yearly lost, to the exceeding detriment of St Petersburg in point of merchandise and especially of provisions …

John Deane suffered the humiliation and danger of his new post and hazardous route for a year.

In 1721 the war with Sweden ended. Never again replicating the martial highs of the Battle of Hango Head, the Russian navy had nevertheless proved itself in an attritional campaign of raids, skirmishes and captured prizes. The war eased itself into a settlement at Nystead that heavily favoured Russian interests in the Baltic. To celebrate, Peter the Great offered amnesty to all disgraced officers. To some the amnesty was a restoration to the tsar's good graces. Robert Little was given his former rank back. To others it was simply a cessation of punishment; technical clemency but no real forgiveness. In 1722 John Deane was set free but ordered to leave Russia and told never to return. His disgrace was total and complete but for one last concession from his sole Russian benefactor. Admiral Apraxin extended a kindness to John Deane that would last him the length of his days. The Admiral gave the Englishman another passport that formally referred to him as 'Captain John Deane'. Apraxin had handed Deane his rank back. Deane had had the most important element of his status restored to him by the one Russian about whom he had nothing bad to say.

John Deane returned to England. He had little in the way of material possessions. His reputation had been destroyed for a second time. Russia had promised a form of exorcism for Boon Island. But when all was said and done, John Deane had simply exchanged one funereal world of wind and ice for another. Yet the twice-exiled Englishman could still call himself Captain John Deane. He also knew the power of the written word. Ink on paper had blunted the disgrace of Boon Island. Ink might yet mitigate against the bankruptcy of almost a decade wasted in the service of a fickle empire. Captain John Deane returned to England full of bile and malice, and a will to convert years of hatred into a written document. Unlike his account of the Boon Island episode, what Deane wrote next would not be for public consumption. It was for a few select eyes and would take him back to Russia clothed in the diplomatic mantle of his home nation.

10

A History of the Russian Fleet

The name of John Deane's document was: *History of the Russian Fleet during the Reign of Peter the Great*. The early pages of the document relayed in a condensed fashion the initial prototypes and failures of Peter the Great's fledgling navy. Deane summed up the tsar's various experiments prior to his tour of Europe with a degree of facetious restraint, stating that, 'to pass them by in silence is the highest compliment'. Deane moved with similar brevity through Peter the Great's trip to Western Europe and his harvest of, and preference for, foreign naval talent. Deane wrote briefly of the early living and working conditions that Peter the Great provided for his foreign employees, the first ships built after his tour of Europe and the tsar's intimate involvement in the construction process of his new fleet. The tsar's war with the Turks and his conflict with his sister were given a cursory mention. But once the document reached the events of 1703, the pace of Deane's narrative slowed down. Deane's principal task for the majority of *The History of the Russian Fleet* was to systematically chart the progress of the war at sea with Sweden. Deane relayed each Russian success and setback. He charted the evolution of Russian naval tactics from the primitive galley victory at Hango Head to the sophisticated deployment of frigates and men-of-war and the judicious use of privateers. As Deane brought his account of each successive year of campaigning to a halt, he would disclose an inventory of warships in the Russian fleet. John Deane's narrative ended in 1722, a year after the peace treaty at Nystead. The majority of this part of the document was relatively clinical and detached. But Deane was not averse to a little editorialising flavoured by more than a touch of righteous anger and contempt. Here Deane describes a galley raid perpetrated by one of the tsar's Italian mercenaries:

> Five large Holland flyboats, arriving at Helsingfors to load timber, were all burned, and the men either killed or wounded in a barbarous manner by Count de Buss, rearadmiral of the Russian galleys, merely through ignorance and indistinction of the neutral flags and passes. This action was utterly unjustifiable …

Deane was not only interested in revealing Russian strength and tactics. He sought also to give an impression of the men that commanded Peter the Great's navy. Throughout the document John Deane would continue to deliver generally critical and occasionally complimentary comments about fellow officers. Sometimes he would arrest the narrative completely for a potted biography and analysis of important high-ranking foreign and Russian officers in the tsar's employ.

John Deane wrote about the Norwegian admiral of the blue, Cornelius Cruys:

> This gentleman, a native of Norway, bred a sailor in Holland and advanced there, had in the last Dutch war been pretty active in privateering upon the English. Some little prejudices imbibed in his youth, through the ill understanding betwixt the two nations, did not easily wear, and might probably render him less a friend to the English than otherwise he would have been. However, he is a man of sobriety and a good seaman; and not withstanding some errors of judgement, has been of excellent service to the Tsar, indefatigably studying to improve the maritime affairs in opposition to the many difficulties industriously thrown in his way, out of envy to him as a foreigner, by the malevolent Russians.

John Deane also wrote about the Danish rear admiral of the blue, Peter Sievers:

He is a man of excellent sense, general knowledge and very exact and methodical in all his conduct; speaks and writes most European tongues; many Russians of distinction will assure you, not a man of their own nation understands their language so well as he. These qualifications render him of great importance; besides he is a bold man; and during the time the ships lie in harbour, in dividing the officers and men &c, has refused to suffer Rear Admiral Gordon to be present at the opening, or consulted upon the execution of orders, even when desired by the Tsar.

Both assessments of both officers were largely positive but both contained broadsides against those that John Deane perceived to be venal and incompetent; the 'malevolent Russians' and Sievers old enemy Thomas Gordon. In the Sievers analysis there was also implied criticism of the tsar's poor judgment in favouring Gordon over Sievers and implicit praise for Deane's own saviour Apraxin, the 'general admiral' referred to in the text.

Once Deane had concluded his account of the campaign the rest of the document took the form of a study of the infrastructures, administration and command structures of the Russian fleet. In these sections Deane's own opinions and prejudices were on more prominent display. He also provided a window into the many brutal social divisions within the Babel-like community of mercenaries, as well as those that still existed in Russian society. Deane began the concluding sections of the document by assessing the galley fleet. The largely Italian and Greek mercenaries that made up the bulk of the galley fleet were pariahs to the rest of the Russian fleet: 'The officers of the men-of-war seldom care to converse much with these people; partly on account of their different languages and manner of living; but more out of abhorrence of the great barbarities they have sometimes practised upon an enemy ... .'

Deane listed the officers' rates of pay and the gratuities included besides pay. Deane listed the falling rates of exchange between shillings and roubles and the gifts and the bounties afforded to admirals. Having praised him earlier in the document John Deane blamed Vice-Admiral Cruys for the poor rates of pay available to foreign officers.

Deane turned his attention to warrant officers and seamen and afforded himself a run of invective against his favourite target, the Russians. Deane's opinion of the under officers was a qualified disrespect. He ascribed their poor quality to bad treatment from their lieutenants who were by and large 'Russians and men of little worth...' Deane went on to attack the general level of Russian seamanship. He put the Russian allergy to naval life down to 'an aversion to the sea' in the makeup of the recruitment pool, whom he described as 'sons of such and such' obliged to serve but with no interest or inclination to do so. Deane also credited a severe decadence of lifestyle to the average Russian officer that neutered their usefulness as navy material, men who 'having credit at large, launched out into all manner of effeminate and extravagant living, frequenting the play-houses ... not caring how little they went to sea ...' Deane blamed the Russian winter for arresting the repetitive drill necessary for maintaining maritime skill and knowledge. Once winter fell everything was forced to stop. Once the ice had thawed the fledgling seamen had forgotten most of what they had learned the previous summer and spring.

John Deane blamed Russian religion as a force that obstructed progress and threatened lives in Peter the Great's navy. Deane relayed a chilling and tragic phenomenon:

> ... their religion enjoins a strict observation of three annual fasts, amounting in the whole to fifteen weeks, besides every Wednesday and Friday throughout the year; and so tenacious is the ignorant superstitious multitude of this less essential part, that great numbers of sick have been landed abroad the Russian fleet, especially in these fasting seasons, and the Tsar has ordered a provision of fresh meat and set a guard to prevent the introducing all other support, many have actually perished rather than violate their ill-informed consciences in eating prohibited viands.

Deane described the early days of Peter the Great's new capital in his document. The importance of the city to the tsar was paramount.

Deane believed that in the city's infancy the tsar 'would have willingly condescended to deliver up all his conquests, upon condition of reserving to himself St Petersburg'. Deane's attitude toward the city seemed to be one of incredulity, not quite believing that anybody could have the hubris to undertake such a building project. He described the ground around St Petersburg as a 'morass and wilderness, producing little or nothing for the support of man'. In Deane's opinion the ground needed to be cultivated in order to produce food for the city's population but the tsar forbade it, prohibiting 'the cutting up of the least tree or shrub within twenty, and in some parts within thirty miles thereof'. Deane noted the city's indefensibility. According to Deane, St Petersburg, 'being built on several islands and standing on a vast extent of ground, will not possibly admit of fortifications'. Deane noted the city's flammability, St Petersburg buildings being mostly made of wood. According to Deane, St Petersburg's best chance of defending itself lay in 'rendering the avenues impassable'. In making this observation Deane afforded himself another opportunity to assault the character of the Russian military. He reasoned that such a tactic suited 'admirably well with the temper of the Russian soldiery, ever reputed better at ambuscade, or defence of a place where they lie covered, than in the bravery of an open assault'. In saying this, John Deane was effectively calling the Russian soldiers cowards.

Deane wrote down his thoughts on the function and deployment of the Russian navy now that the war with Sweden had ended. In peacetime the priority of Peter the Great was to establish trade treaties, 'to obtain the privilege of exporting, in his own ships, the product of his own dominions'. Then there was the problem of England and Holland. Now that the war was over the two technically friendly nations were likely to take offence at the fact that Peter the Great was 'victualling his ships at much cheaper rates than they'. There was also the question of monopoly. The spoils of the recent war had 'drawn in a manner, the whole commerce of his dominion into the Baltic; and necessitated the general system of Russian imports and exports'. Deane suspected that the tsar would exempt his own ships from paying tolls. Peter the Great also had plans to connect his provinces internally by canals, further improving trade. The tsar's next great horizon was to 'grasp into his hands the Persian trade'. Deane concluded this section of the document by predicting that the tsar wanted, 'a port in the hithermost parts of the Baltic for the bringing these designs to maturity', but encouraged whoever might read his report that the tsar's plans were 'as yet but in embryo …'.

Deane wrote of rumours of the tsar's plans to send his fleet to the Mediterranean, the possibility of further conflict with the Turks, the benefit of such a campaign to a still inexperienced navy and the danger to Peter the Great of mass desertions once his men saw, 'the preferable standards of living in other countries …'. Deane gave details of Russian galley building and timber transportation. He wrote how frequently Peter the Great would need to replace his ships to maintain its strength. Deane conceded the strong possibility that Peter the Great could indeed build a navy to match and dominate the Swedes and the Danes. John Deane compared the command structures of the Russian navy with the English navy. He foresaw problems for the tsar when Russians were promoted above their levels of competence, an endemic problem in the Russian navy. Deane appeared to abate his blanket denunciation of Russians for a sentence or two by conceding that, 'There are some men of capacity among the Russians,' but couldn't resist stating that, 'foreigners ever desire to leave 'em ashore …'. Deane believed that the Russians struggled to sail well in bad weather and that an 'inferior force' could 'attack and destroy' them if they engaged the Russians during a 'strong gale of wind'.

Deane seemed be to working up a head of steam for a page-long rant about Russian incompetence. The specific context for the rant was the ill treatment and humiliation of any foreigner who had the nerve to gainsay the tsar in matters of naval wisdom regarding handling a ship in foul weather. Deane's riposte gave full vent to the barely suppressed hatred he felt for his former paymasters and the nominally latent contempt he had for the majority of his peers, Russian cowardice and incompetence being the two frequent and recurrent gobs of venom spat by Captain John Deane from the pages of his document at Peter the Great's indigenous subordinates:

And how much less will they be able to do it, after ten or twelve days' continuance at sea, when many are seasick, or otherwise in ill state of health, and the rest thunderstruck with terror of an approaching engagement [...] The officers from a sense of their people's inexperience will be fearful of opening their ports or loosening their guns, lest by ill steerage, or other mismanagement, the sea run in at their portholes, or the guns break loose and endanger their sinking, especially among the Russians, whose known property is ever to recoil from danger, even when immediate presence of mind is requisite to repel an otherwise unavoidable ruin [...] And even in calm moderate weather, when the people are in condition to behave something better, yet the enemy has great advantage through the badness of their powder; and commanders acquainted with the hazard they run, above all things dread the blowing up of their ships, through the fear, ignorance and confusion of the undisciplined multitude.

The storm in Deane seemed to blow itself out somewhat for the concluding pages of the document. Deane reported on the Russian ironworks, the peacetime fate of his own last great vessel, the *Devonshire*, which had become a transport ship for weapons, ammunition, wax and paper. He reported on details of disputes between officers regarding matters of advancement and pay. He wrote about building work, new ships, further disputations, strategy, deployment and trade. Deane concluded his document with a detailed inventory of the Russian fleet and its officers. His final observations of Peter the Great's prospects as a naval superpower were sober and critical:

I am fully of the opinion though the number of his ships is increased, yet his seamen, properly so called, are not more numerous, within these last four years. And the vast charge he is yearly at to discipline his men and keep his fleet to its present height, whilst or no service is done him in return of such expense, much inevitably exhaust his treasures and render him less formidable. All future designs and expectations must abide in a state of inexecution till his affairs in Asia stand on a less precarious footing; and should he in turn meet with adverse fortune, it would past all peradventure ruin many if not most of his undertakings.

It was a back-handed compliment to Peter the Great. John Deane acknowledged that the Russian navy, for better or worse, was held together by the industry and will of the tsar. The project's success would perish if its architect were to die suddenly. It was an astute and prophetic observation. Deane's once prospective saviour turned author of his present torment, died an agonising death a year later from an infected bladder. The potency of his navy died with him.

But where was John Deane in his own document? And to what extent did the 'Shadow Man of Boon Island' truly reveal himself?

Unlike his accounts of the New England shipwreck, John Deane relegated himself to a supporting player in the wider narrative of Peter the Great's maritime adventure. Deane did not put his name to the document. The authorship was ascribed to 'A Contemporary Englishman'. Deane appeared to give no more weight to his own exploits than he did to numerous others that sailed and fought along-side him. He referred to himself in the third person. He seemed to so divorce himself from the sailor named John Deane he was writing about as to give no indication that the author and the sailor were one and the same person. To confuse matters even further, he made passing reference to another John Deane who worked for Peter the Great as a master builder. Long after he had died, future readers of the anonymous document would assume that the two John Deane's were the same person. Deane relayed his own campaigning career with a detachment that seemed to indicate the desire for anonymity. Yet Deane was careful to justify his role in the Kronslot disaster and made sure that the reader understood where the blame ought to lie. Deane also omitted crucial information about himself. There was no mention in the document of the incident at the Gulf of Danzig where Deane was forced to hand over the two merchantmen to the English and the Dutch. There was no mention of the subsequent court martial and Deane's commuted sentence transporting timber from Kazan. The only reference to John Deane's expulsion from Russia was oblique.

In his final inventory of all the commanding officers that had served the tsar in the Baltic campaign, Deane listed his own name. The entry simply reads: 'Deane, John; England; Captain, dismissed in 1722.'

Although John Deane could have made a decent fist of trying to vindicate himself, he elected not to. Back in England he was still a notorious man, now newly disgraced and touting for employment. It did not do well to advertise his failures any more than he had to, even if a compelling case could be made that his second fall from grace was not his fault. Whereas Deane was the fallible but essentially competent and benign saviour of his own Boon Island narratives, in *The History of the Russian Fleet* John Deane's tactic seemed to have been to hide in plain sight.

For those looking for evidence of John Deane's personality and character, the document seemed to raise more questions than it satisfactorily answered. But what it did appear to do was inadvertently clear up many of the accusations that had been levelled against Deane by Christopher Langman and company in New England. Among other things, Langman had accused Deane of being incompetent, a coward and incapable of commanding loyalty in his men. Anybody reading *A History of the Russian Fleet* would have been left with very little doubt that John Deane was a very skilled sailor. Throughout the document a thorough knowledge of seamanship was wielded casually and sometimes even used as a weapon to illuminate the incompetence of others. Deane's military record denoted a cunning and talented sailor. His competence was even used against him when his enemies tried to lay the blame of the loss of the *Portsmouth* and the *London* at his feet. That Deane survived so long and captured so many prizes in seas far more dangerous than New England's coastal waters, fighting in an experimental war against an experienced enemy, was a living rebuke against Langman's second accusation, that John Deane was a coward. And had Deane elected to include the details of his court martial in the document, the example of the crew of the *Samson*'s vindication of Deane would have put paid to Langman's third accusation, that Deane was a tyrant incapable of inspiring loyalty in his men.

Whether through a pragmatic form of guile or genuine fair-mindedness, in his Boon Island narratives Deane had been surprisingly fair to his enemies. Such chivalry was completely absent from *A History of the Russian Fleet*. For the majority of the document he tried to maintain an air of detachment. His prose was mostly condensed, stripped down and systematic. But a bubble of vitriol would break the surface and the wounded man was visible underneath. Once the constraints of writing the narrative of the war with Sweden had been lifted and the document became a series of critiques of Russia's various naval practices, Deane felt less reason to be restrained, giving fuller vent to years of accumulated resentment and humiliation. In *A History of the Russian Fleet* John Deane was most clearly visible in his hatred.

Part Three

Spy

11

Townsend

When Captain John Deane returned to England he circulated his document among the powerful and the influential. Deane was touting for work, demonstrating his detailed knowledge of Russian maritime matters in the hope that it could be converted into some remunerative office or post. The document was read by Charles Townsend, the 3rd Viscount Townsend, the second most powerful politician in the ruling Whig Party, who would soon become John Deane's new mentor and the greatest benefactor he would ever know.

Viscount Townsend was Robert Walpole's right-hand man. Walpole was the most contentious British political genius of his age. He was the leader of the Whig Party. His official office was first lord of the treasury and chancellor of the exchequer but Walpole was the first ever party leader to be referred to by the title 'prime minister'. The sobriquet was initially a term of abuse devised by Walpole's enemies but it soon passed into common usage as the title given to the leader of the governing political party. Walpole was a hated man. He was the target of the best artists, playwrights and poets in an era saturated by caustic, brilliant and merciless satirists. Walpole was accused of cronyism and corruption. He was censorious and a ruthless and often vindictive enemy. But Robert Walpole's intervention had saved Britain from financial catastrophe when government sponsored over-investment in the South Sea Company led to near financial collapse. More than any other event in his long political career, the resolution of the 'Bursting of the South Sea Bubble', as the disaster came to be known, secured Walpole's position for the next two decades. But prior to the South Sea crisis, Robert Walpole's ascent had been troubled and precarious. And sharing his hardships had been his childhood friend and closest political ally, Charles Townsend.

Both men were born in Norfolk. Walpole's family was wealthy but Townsend's was rich and titled. The Townsends of Raynham became the pre-eminent family in the region after the fall of James II. The Townsends were Protestant and occupied the vacuum created by a prominent Catholic family, whose base of power evaporated when

Charles Townsend, the third Viscount Townsend. John Deane's second great mentor employed and protected Deane during his lengthy career as diplomat and spy for the Walpole administration. *Illustration by Jean Nightingale*

their Papist monarch fled the country. Walpole and Townsend studied at Eton together. They became close friends. Townsend would later marry Walpole's sister Dorothy, further strengthening their bond. The two men entered politics and joined the Whig party. Their fortunes fluctuated as they navigated the precarious temperaments of a rapid succession of monarchs. Their fledgling years were vulnerable. They were Whigs in a predominantly Tory environment. Townsend clashed with Queen Anne over the question of succession. Walpole was impeached for corruption and imprisoned in the Tower of London. Although the accession of George I broke the back of Tory opposition as the king, hostile to the Tories' perceived anti-Hanoverian politics, sought to reduce their majority, the new monarch brought his own set of problems with him. Walpole and Townsend were troubled by George I's tendency to use British money and resources to further his own dynastic interests on the continent. And though Walpole and Townsend had no enemies of significance in opposition, the Whig party was ulcerated with factions. Townsend was one of two secretaries of state. The fact that James Stanhope, the other secretary of state, despised Townsend and was favoured by the king undermined what should have been a strong alliance with Walpole. Tensions between Townsend and the king saw him demoted from secretary of state and given the humiliating post of lieutenant of Ireland before being dismissed from office altogether in 1716. Robert Walpole resigned in protest. The reclamation of the nation's finances in the wake of the Bursting of the South Sea Bubble planted Walpole in a position of virtually unassailable power and terminally discredited his enemies who had largely encouraged investment in the doomed venture. Walpole promoted Townsend to the position of northern secretary of state, where he thrived.

As a political double act, Walpole and Townsend complemented one another. Walpole was shrewd but could be abrasive and ruthless. He was hated by his enemies and was not always liked by his allies. Although he could be imperious, Townsend was the softer of the two men, better liked, more affable and an important tempering influence to Walpole's sharper edges. Many filial bonds held Walpole and

Townsend together in this, the golden age of their professional partnership. But both men were equally united in fear of a great mutual enemy: Jacobitism.

In 1668 the English king, James II, had converted to Catholicism. His change of faith was initially tolerated. But for what remained of his reign the king set about what was perceived to be an incremental catholicising of the country as laws were challenged and Catholics were appointed to key government positions. The king, from his perspective, was simply trying to create a level playing field where Catholic and Protestant had equal status under the law. But the king's incrementalism soon gave way to a force-feeding of pro-Catholic reform that turned his own people against him. The king unwittingly created an open door for the Dutch Protestant monarch William of Orange to sail up the Thames and take the English throne without a shot being fired in protest by James II's own army and navy.

The transition was not without deferred bloodshed. There were followers of James on British soil who were willing to take up arms. They were called Jacobites after 'Jacobus', the Latin translation of the name James. There would be a Jacobite rebellion in 1715 that was not fully suppressed until the following year.

James II was still alive and resided in France. He had the sympathy of Catholic Europe and a core of loyal exiles who dreamed of invasion and a second restoration of the Stuart monarchy. And when James II died that core of loyalty transferred to his son, who was called the 'Pretender' by his enemies and James III by the faithful.

Walpole and Townsend were ever alert to the prospect of Stuart plots and conspiracies, the worst manifestation of which would be a foreign-backed Jacobite invasion of Great Britain. Walpole and Townsend had their spies dotted throughout Europe, but Russia was something of a blind spot. And Russia was becoming a concern since the death of Peter the Great. There were disquieting rumours that the Jacobites were gathering strength and influence in the court of the new Russian monarch. Experienced eyes and ears were needed in St Petersburg.

Despite the relatively benign presence of Admiral Norris' squadron in the Baltic during the Great Northern War, as the conflict between Russia and Sweden had come to be known, George I and Peter the Great despised one another. When the war began, relations between the British and the Russians had been cordial. William and Mary reigned in England. William had even made a present of a yacht to the young tsar. But Peter the Great had little love for the House of Hanover as it replaced the House of Orange on the throne of Great Britain. When the tsar died, George I had hoped to take advantage of what he believed would be an inevitable downturn in Russian influence in European affairs. He anticipated Britain would fill the breach. But events in 1725 scotched British ambition and made her international footing precarious. The choice of a bride for a French king had caused a ripple effect that threatened to leave Britain in a vulnerable position. The Spanish had presented their Infanta as a prospective wife for Louis XV. He was not interested. Spain was offended. With a potential alliance sundered, Spain needed an ally to protect it against France. Spain looked to Austria. A Spanish/Austrian alliance was hostile to British interests. France's actions provoked a succession of alliances and counter alliances that left Britain in the cold and in need of allies lest it leave itself exposed to potential enemies in the north and south of the continent. It was time to make friendly overtures toward Russia and persuade it to make compatriots of Britain and France. Britain's choice of diplomat was a Frenchman named Campredon. He approached the Russian court and made a hash of negotiations, pushing the Russian royal family further into the arms of George I's enemies.

A new problem was the tsarina. With Peter the Great gone, his widow Catherine ruled. Catherine I only reigned for two years, but in that small amount of time she managed to generate a disproportionate amount of grief and anxiety for Britain. The chief cause of tension was her favouring of the House of Holstein. Peter the Great had married his daughter to the Duke of Holstein-Gottorp. The Duke held enormous sway at the Russian court in St Petersburg. Holstein hated George I because of a disputed territory held by the Hanoverians. Holstein ensured that the bad blood between the tsar and the British monarchy was held over into the new administration.

Campredon's failure only exacerbated old hatreds. Holstein and Catherine embraced the British-born enemies of George I. St Petersburg was now more of a haven for Jacobites than it had ever been. But the news didn't seem to have rattled British cages as much as it should have done. Certainly in the early months of Catherine I's reign, few prominent British politicians took her seriously. The exception was Townsend. A reliable and knowledgeable man in St Petersburg was now essential. Townsend had recently read a document by an observant and disgruntled mercenary who had fought for the dead tsar for a decade and seemed to loathe Jacobites as much as he did. Townsend arranged to meet the anonymous author of *A History of the Russian Fleet*.

Viscount Townsend persuaded Captain John Deane to go back to Russia. Deane's official title was to be the new consul of British governancy. He was supposed to salve the tensions between Britain and Russia by encouraging trade, but his real purpose was to gather intelligence about the levels of antipathy among the Russians toward the British.

12

Who Sent You Here?

*J*ohn Deane was torn between a sense of duty, a need to advance and deep disquiet in his gut about revisiting the place that had, in its own way, damaged and tormented him as much as Boon Island ever did. Later, when Deane had come back from Russia, he would write a candid letter to Townsend admitting the levels of anxiety he had felt and how near he had come to refusing to go:

> It was not without great reluctance that I engaged in that affair having formerly experienced the malice of that set of men. But as it was impossible for any person not present to believe with what bitterness they had persecuted me in Russia, so I could not absolutely refuse going.

John Deane would last a scant sixteen days in his new post before being expelled from Russia a second time.

The three years between the end of John Deane's first Russian adventure and the beginning of his disastrous second are another of the numerous black spaces in his biography during which virtually nothing is known about his life. The unassailable facts are that he was recruited by Townsend and that he married. John Deane's marriage, presumably the most intimate and personal venture he ever embarked upon, yields virtually nothing in the way of illumination. In the chaotic, intermittently well-documented sprawl of John Deane's existence his spouse remained something of an 'Ahab's wife' figure. Her first name is known. She was called Sarah. But her maiden name cannot be determined without a degree of guesswork.

In 1722 a Sarah Hughes married a John Deane in St Mary Somerset Church, in the City of London. Whether this was the Captain John Deane of Boon Island and St Petersburg cannot be absolutely determined. Other than her name, the possible date of her wedding and the date of her death, little else is known about Sarah Deane. And so Sarah Deane joined the better, deeper part of the captain, invisible in the shadows of his own story.

By late May, John Deane was a passenger onboard a ship bound for Kronslot. On 26 May 1725 the ship docked for a short while at Elsinore, where Deane observed three Russian ships that were bound for Spain. He tried to glean information about the ships from 'a resident'. He wrote to Townsend telling the Viscount what he had seen. Deane was not impressed with the condition of the Russian ships, calling them 'good for nothing'.

John Deane reached Kronslot on 2 June. His first impression of Russia was somewhat ominous and oddly apocalyptic. He saw, 'lying in the road and in all appearance fit for sea, eleven sail ships of the line and two frigates'.

Deane was forbidden to come ashore straight away. Customs were required to come aboard and find out the names and destinations of all the ships passengers. Deane was kept waiting for hours. He observed Kronslot. He was surprised at the state of disrepair. There was still so much building work that needed to be done. What surprised Deane even more was the multitude of soldiers sitting idle when they could have been employed on repairs to the haven.

While Deane was waiting he made a potentially pleasant discovery: Lord High Admiral Count Apraxin had arrived in Kronslot the previous evening. Accompanying him were Vice Admirals Sievers and Gordon as well as Wilster a Danish vice admiral, Captain Commodore Ivan Sinavin and Rear Admiral of the White Thomas Saunders. The assembly of familiar high-ranking naval warriors was a combustible mixture of dear friends, sympathetic allies and hated enemies. John Deane was anxious to deliver the news that he had returned to Russia to Apraxin himself rather than have the information reach him via an old adversary. It was a moot concern. The news appeared to have already reached the lord high admiral. His ship, the *Alexander*, anchored and visible from the deck of John Deane's vessel, signalled to Deane via the raising of a flag. A pinnace was dispatched and a delegate from the *Alexander* requested that Captain John Deane accompany him. Deane climbed aboard the pinnace, which ferried the English captain across the small stretch of water to the *Alexander*. Deane climbed aboard and was led into a room. Waiting for him was Apraxin, Sievers and Thomas Saunders. Apraxin saluted John Deane. His tone was warm and his manner was kind. He asked Deane what he was doing back in Russia.

'I have bought some good news over to dispose of, and if found a prospect of things answering, probably might settle on trade and remain sometime in Russia,' Deane replied.

Apraxin was not convinced. He gently challenged John Deane, stating that it was his personal belief that his former protégé 'had other affairs in hand' and that he should 'tell the truth' and produce his 'credentials of commission'.

John Deane stood by his initial story.

Apraxin advised that if Deane did not produce some form of official documentation, the lord high admiral would be obliged to use him ill.

Apraxin sent Deane back to his vessel with instructions to wait until the lord high admiral received orders as to what to do with him.

John Deane ruminated on an ostensibly friendly but loaded and tense exchange with the Russian aristocrat. Despite the implied threat of violence from an old friend, Deane was more concerned with having offended Apraxin than any 'ill usage' he had promised. Deane wanted to speak to Apraxin alone, out of the earshot of Saunders in particular, a Jacobite who in Deane's estimation, 'hated His Majesty, the government and me in particular'. But Deane feared that insisting on a private conversation with the lord high admiral would make him look even more suspicious than he already did.

A day later John Deane stood before Apraxin, Sievers and Saunders for the second time. Deane showed Apraxin the only official piece of documentation he possessed, his commission. Saunders took the commission from Apraxin and read it for himself. He was not satisfied.

Saunders asked Apraxin whether John Deane's 'coming in such a character had been notified by the British to the Russian Court?'

'No,' Apraxin said.

Saunders began to ridicule Deane saying that Deane's status 'ought not to be regarded'.

Deane had had enough and interrupted Saunders as he was speaking. The two Englishmen's tempers flared and something of a slanging match ensued. Whether the argument was conducted in English or Russian is not clear. John Deane's Russian was better than Saunders's. Deane used his superior Russian to his advantage and tried to justify the manner of his sending 'without notification' to Apraxin, in Saunder's presence, trusting that his enemy wouldn't fully comprehend his meaning. Deane entreated Apraxin to keep his arrival secret for short while. Apraxin appeared to Deane 'a little pleased' with his outburst. He congratulated Deane and asked Deane to visit him again before the Englishman travelled to St Petersburg. Apraxin called his secretary. He instructed the secretary to write a letter of endorsement to Catherine I. The letter stated that John Deane had served Russia and had been discharged three years earlier at Apraxin's request. Deane and Apraxin agreed to meet the following morning.

John Deane returned to the *Alexander* at four o'clock. He may have had to wait a few hours for the admiral to surface. Since the death of Peter the Great, Apraxin was prone to sleep in till six or seven o'clock in the morning. When the two men eventually met for the second time, John Deane sought to justify himself in the light of Saunders' animosity and a decade's worth of persecutions. Deane framed his grievances in international terms, his enemies being responsible for preventing, in Deane's words, 'a reconciliation between the two crowns'. Apraxin seemed to agree. He reassured Deane that he gave the captain's enemies' accusations little weight.

'Tho I hear them I don't regard them,' he said. 'You observed that yesterday. I took no notice of Saunders' suggestions, and you know my way better than they do or ever will.'

John Deane noticed what he called 'people of fashion' beginning to arrive onboard the Alexander. Deane mistrusted the new arrivals.

He believed he was being spied upon. He had been caught out by Saunders' interrogation. His arrival in Kronslot had been anticipated and prepared for by his enemies.

Over the next two days Deane spoke with Sievers and Apraxin. He tried to enlist their support in endorsing his credentials so that he might advance to St Petersburg and do the job Townsend had officially instructed him to do. Apraxin reassured Deane that he believed him but could not act fully on his behalf without something in writing from the British government. Apraxin's letter to the Russian court had received no response.

Apraxin spoke alone with John Deane for two hours. It was their most intense and personal discussion since Deane's return. Now Deane was at liberty to speak as freely as he dared. The two men talked about 'the good effects of a reconciliation between the crowns'. The conversation was punctuated by a note of personal affection from Apraxin to Deane. The lord high admiral put his hand to his breast and said to Deane, 'You will always find me Apraxin.' Deane tentatively mentioned the Holstein business. Apraxin was pessimistic saying that the Empress Catherine, 'could not abandon the Duke's interests'. Deane criticised rash 'councils inconsistent with the true interests of Russia,' and encouraged Apraxin to oppose them. Deane told Apraxin that the lord high admiral had the confidence of both Viscount Townsend and King George himself as an internal force for reconciliation between Britain and Russia. Apraxin seemed moved by this. Deane, for his part, told Apraxin that he would never have returned to Russia had he not been confident of the admiral's patronage and begged 'for its continuance' for the duration of his stay. Apraxin agreed to prepare the way for Deane as best he could. There was a succession of people Deane needed to meet: gatekeepers between Deane and the court whose endorsements were crucial if Deane were to achieve his diplomatic ends. Deane had planned to visit Great Chancellor Count Golovkin first. Apraxin advised against this. Golovkin was pro-Holstein and a Jacobite sympathiser. Apraxin encouraged Deane to meet the potentially more sympathetic Count Tolstoi before approaching Golovkin. Apraxin promised he would help the best he could but warned Deane

1   John Deane's birthplace: Wilford village, on the banks of the River Trent. (Mark Nightingale)

2   The ill-fated crew of the *Nottingham Galley* began their journey to New England at Gravesend. (Mark Nightingale)

3   The *Nottingham Galley* accompanied a convoy to Whitby where they sheltered from bad weather. The *Nottingham Galley* broke away from the convoy and carried on to Ireland, alone and unprotected.

4   The Irish port of Killybegs, where John Deane picked up his cargo of butter and cheese. On the Irish coast the *Nottingham Galley* encountered French privateers. (Carol King)

5   The crew of the Nottingham Galley were marooned on Boon Island for twenty-four days. Four men died. One of them was eaten by the survivors. (Image courtesy of the Library of Congress)

6 The shipwreck survivors were fed, clothed and nursed to a semblance of health by the residents of Portsmouth, New England. In Portsmouth, Christopher Langman would formally accuse John Deane of fraud and attempted murder. (Image courtesy of the Library of Congress)

7 Peter the Great.

8 Cleve Severin's statue of Peter the Great overlooks the River Thames at Greenwich, commemorating the Russian tsar's time in London, gleaning maritime knowledge he would use to build the formidable but fractious navy in which John Deane would serve. (Adam Nightingale)

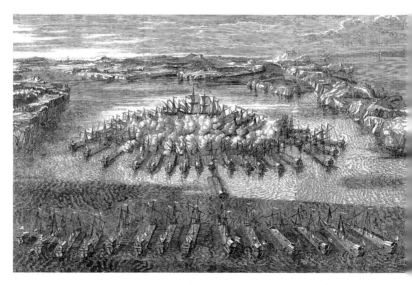

9 The Battle of Hango Head. The key naval victory in Peter the Great's war against Sweden. The battle could not have been won without the help and expertise of foreign mercenaries.

10 Sir Robert Walpole. The British prime minister would rescue John Deane from further disgrace when he employed him as a spy following Deane's court martial in Russia.

11 Pelham Street, Nottingham, where according to local myth John Deane killed his brother in an argument over money. (Mark Nightingale)

GEORGE's COMBAT

From Papal Power and Papal Bills, / From Rebels, Fiends and Romish Bulls, / Our Church sav'd by GEORGE's Hands, / Now in a Rock triumphant stands. / Religion sits beneath at Rest, / Smiles in the Prince in whom She's blest, / Valour combling Truths Supporter, / On Him depending Britain's Sons.

His image rising tho' makes Vary feeble, / His external Breast takes Master dire, / The Arts of Rome, the Pride of Gaul, / Prostrate before their Victor fall. / NASSAU with British thunder arm'd, / Old Lewis, in the World alarm'd, / Great GEORGE improving NASSAU's Plan, / Shall end the Work which he began.

Publish'd according to Act of Parliament

12   Hanoverian propaganda. An illustration showing George II victorious over the dragon of Jacobitism. The exiled supporters of the deposed James II would become John Deane's enemies of choice as he worked as both consul and spy for the Walpole administration. (Image Courtesy of the Library of Congress)

13   Charles Stuart in Derby. In 1745, John Deane's fears of a Jacobite invasion of England took substance when the heir to the Stuart throne arrived in the Midlands with an army of Highlanders. (Mark Nightingale)

14   The Battle of Culloden. The Jacobite threat was obliterated at Culloden in April 1746. John Deane's money helped raise the troops of the Duke of Kingston's 10th Light Horse. Kingston's soldiers would commit terrible atrocities on the Scottish battlefield.

15 The Rock Cemetery in Nottingham (once the sight of Gallows Hill) where a Mr Miller, who perpetrated a violent robbery against the elderly John Deane, was publically hanged. (Mark Nightingale)

16 John Deane's grave in St Wilfrid's cemetery. (Mark Nightingale)

17 A series of illustrations from *John Deane: Historic Adventures by Land and Sea* by
W.H.G. Kingston. The Victorian author perpetuated many myths about John Deane that are still
believed today.

    A.   The young John Deane is shot at by gamekeepers while out poaching.

    B.   John Deane fights cattle thieves while working as a drover's apprentice.

    C.   John Deane unwittingly visits the home of a mercenary embroiled in a Jacobite
        conspiracy to assassinate William of Orange.

    D.   John Deane is held prisoner by pirates.

that his cause would be perpetually on the back foot unless something in writing from Deane's government that officially endorsed his presence in Russia could be produced. As a preliminary measure Apraxin insisted that Deane write something in his own hand stating his intentions. Deane was reluctant but Apraxin insisted. Deane put pen to paper. The letter read:

I whose name is underlined, so declare to his Excellency the General Admiral Apraxin that on the 9th of May last part, the Right Honourable the Lord Viscount Townsend did give me permission when a favourable opportunity should present to signify to his Excellency that His Majesty the King of Great Britain was at all times ready to come to a reconciliation with Her Majesty of Russia, and that both His Majesty as well as Lord Townsend would take all opportunities of expressing their gratefulness of his Excellency's goodness showed to such of His Majesty's subjects as obtained a due sense of their allegiance to their lawful sovereign whilst under his Excellency's command.

Privately John Deane agonised over the potentially difficult position the unsanctioned letter put him in. He worried that having appeased one benefactor in agreeing to Apraxin's gentle demand he had offended another in going beyond the authority ceded to him by Townsend. Deane left the letter with Apraxin and returned to his own boat. Apraxin sent his steward to Count Tolstoi to prepare the way for Captain John Deane.

Deane had yet to set foot on Russian soil and his mission had already been severely compromised. He had made a tactical blunder by refusing to present his commission to Saunders when he demanded to see it. One can only assume that animosity had prevented Deane from putting his old enmities aside and taking a more pragmatic course of action for the sake of his mission. As far as Deane was concerned, the mistake had earned him the initial suspicion of Admiral Apraxin. What had saved him was the old affection between the two men. But Apraxin was still a servant of Russia and Deane's behaviour had been suspicious. In Deane's own mind, despite the genuine bond between the two men, the only way he could secure Apraxin's support was to write a letter he had no authority to write. And much as Deane would question his own actions in those first few days his situation would have been greatly improved had Townsend given him official documentation. Townsend was not incompetent, inexperienced in foreign affairs or negligent, but the oversight seemed foolish. It appeared that Townsend had gambled on Deane's quiet entry into Russia. Deane was supposed to have approached Apraxin secretly and talked with initial freedom, one ally to another, about a cause to which both men were sympathetic. Apraxin was to have paved the way for Deane in St Petersburg, accruing allies for reconciliation between Russia and Great Britain before internal tensions could escalate and lines were publicly drawn in the sand. Diplomatic papers were seemingly unnecessary. As far as Townsend was concerned Deane was his own flesh and blood epistle, known and read by Apraxin through years of faithful prior service. But Deane's first meeting had been anything but secret. Saunders had been there and his presence and immediate challenge had changed the nature of the negotiations. It had placed a barrier in front of Apraxin that the admiral could not afford to overlook.

Deane was beginning to realise that Saunders' presence was clearly not a coincidence. Saunders had known that Deane was coming. Deane was aware that he had been closely observed, at least from the moment his ship had entered Kronslot and possibly even before that. Part of Townsend's brief to John Deane had been to 'transmit whatever intelligence he may be able to get for His Majesty's service'. The presence and foreknowledge of so many enemies in Kronslot was crucial and disturbing information that fed into Deane and Townsend's worst fears; that Jacobites were embedded in Russian affairs, powerful and organised with sophisticated networks of intelligence.

Although Deane's experience and knowledge of Russian affairs was peerless, the levels of hatred that still festered towards him potentially neutered any advantage Townsend may have hoped to gain by employing him as the king's man in Russia. It seems impossible to imagine Townsend being so naive as to misjudge Russian animosity to Deane's advent so disastrously. The hostile reception did not surprise John Deane. He had not wanted to come back to Russia. He was perfectly aware of the animosity that still existed toward him: 'It was impossible for any person not present to believe with what bitterness they had persecuted me'. The problem seemed to reside in Deane's paymasters refusing to believe him, or else John Deane's own reluctance to tell them the entire truth for fear of not being believed.

John Deane prepared to leave Kronslot and meet Count Tolstoi. Deane's departure was further delayed, which afforded him another opportunity to talk to Apraxin. Captain Commodore Peter Bredale was present for a short while. Deane seemed to like Bredale, for the Norwegian had opposed Ivan Sinavin, a Russian whom Deane had particularly despised. When Bredale left the room, Apraxin and Deane's conversation became more intimate and personal. Both men drank coffee together. Deane admitted that his previous adventures in Russia had given him grey hairs. Apraxin talked of the grief he felt at the recent death of a beloved nephew. He wept as he talked.

On 5 June John Deane left for shore in a pinnace accompanied by Apraxin's servant. The ever-petulant Russian weather flared up once again. The pinnace was forced to put Deane ashore at a nearby village. Deane spent the night in the village. In the morning he rode to meet Count Tolstoi on horseback.

Tolstoi's reception was polite but not exactly warm. Deane presented Tolstoi with his commission. Tolstoi already had a copy of the letter Deane had written at Apraxin's request, translated from English into Russian.

'We are not in peace with England,' Tolstoi said, 'and I cannot tell what to think of admitting a consul.'

'I had not heard of there being war with England,' Deane replied.

Tolstoi and Deane drank brandy together, after which Deane left for St Petersburg.

One of Tolstoi's servants had instructed Apraxin's servant to take Deane to see Count Golovkin as soon as he entered St Petersburg. The Russian capital was ten miles from Tolstoi's residence. John Deane arrived in St Petersburg at noon. Deane had arranged to stay with an old friend, a Welsh engineer and shipbuilder named Joseph Ney. Deane's baggage had not yet arrived. Barely settled in St Petersburg, Deane went to see Golovkin.

Convincing Golovkin of his credibility was always going to be a tall order for John Deane. Deane knew Golovkin and disliked him intensely. To Deane, Golovkin was a 'tool of the Jacobites' and 'a man of moderate parts', 'inclined to luxury' and 'indolence'. By the time Golovkin had finished with Deane, the English captain would promote the Russian chancellor to the exalted status of, 'my professed enemy'.

Golovkin did not receive John Deane straight away. Deane met Privy Counsellor Vasilley Stepanoff instead. Stepanoff spoke to Apraxin's servant before speaking to Deane. Then Stepanoff asked Deane two direct questions. How long had Deane served in Russia? How long had he been away from Russia? Deane answered that he had served eleven years and been absent for three years. Deane was instructed to come back to the College of Foreign Affairs the following day.

The next day the privy counsellor asked Deane where he was currently staying. Deane told him. Deane was dismissed. It was 7 June. John Deane heard nothing more from Stepanoff until 14 June.

Deane made daily trips to the Customs House to enquire about his baggage, which was still missing. He wrote to Townsend, who was in Hanover with the king. He sent the letter via a trusted friend at Danzig. All the time Deane was aware that he was being watched and made certain not to visit anybody he knew that might arouse further suspicion.

The week or so of silence gave John Deane time to observe the new Russia at closer quarters. The country was in a state of official mourning for the dead tsar. But as John Deane wandered around St Petersburg, he saw little evidence of real sorrow. In Deane's opinion, Peter the Great did not seem greatly missed by the populace that he had dragged into modernity. Deane devised a crude litmus test to determine if there were any people that genuinely grieved for the tsar. When in conversation, Deane would mention the tsar's name, 'several times in discourse on purpose' and 'neither saw a tear' nor 'heard a sigh at the mentioning of his name among the Russians'.

Deane also had chance to meditate on the nature of the navy Peter the Great had bequeathed his widow. First impressions seemed favourable. What John Deane saw in Kronslot and St Petersburg seemed 'fit for sea', on a cursory viewing. But Deane was not convinced the Russians could put a fleet in the ocean that summer. According to Deane, 'provisions were short' and 'pinnaces were lacking'. The Russians were spending their money on anything but the navy, the one institution that had carved them a place in wider European affairs. For a seasoned naval warrior like John Deane, Kronslot and St Petersburg was a moribund panorama of decay. The Russian ruling elite were allowing their greatest asset to rot from the inside through neglect and misspending. This was good news for Great Britain but there seemed to be a pang of sadness in Deane that something that he had had a hand in creating had been treated so poorly by those who had inherited it.

In that week or so of silence, John Deane's adversaries had been organising themselves. Whereas previously Deane's enemies had been naval officers, now they were predominantly merchants. 'The Factory', the common name for expatriate mercantile organisations, prepared its case against Deane. The Factory's intention was to force Deane out of the capital. It intended to exert its influence at court to have him expelled. It would contact the Russian Factory in London and try to blacken Deane's name there. It planned to utilise its British contacts to draft a bill in parliament protesting Deane's presence in Russia in order to have him recalled. The pretext for John Deane's unsuitability was his past. The Factory planned to dredge up the official version of John Deane's expulsion from Russia, scandalise him afresh and destroy any confidence the court might have had for permitting him to stay in their country.

Five members of the Factory were more conspicuous than others as they poured poison in the ears of prominent Russians regarding John Deane. The five Factory members' names were Nettleton, Vigor, Gardener, Elinsall and Hodgkin. On 13 June all five men were summoned to the College of Foreign Affairs where they were interrogated by Chancellor Iaguzhinsky. The chancellor asked them a series of questions. He wanted to know if the British government sent prior warning of Deane's advent.

The five men answered, 'no'.

He asked if the five representatives of the Factory wanted John Deane among them.

Vigor said that they 'had no manner of occasion'. Hodgkin was more circumspect in his response stating that, 'Such a person might be of service, provided it was one that was acceptable to the court.'

The chancellor was quick to put Hodgkin in his place, reminding him that definitions of acceptability was something 'not asked' of Factory members.

The Chancellor repeated his question to Elinsall.

Elinsall stated that for Deane's presence to be remotely acceptable he had to produce commissions, 'and communicate his instructions as far as concerned them'. Nettleton and Gardener remained mute on the matter.

The five Factory representatives were excused and left.

It was a deceptively tense exchange defined by caution among the Factory with regard to overstating their intentions, and belligerence on the part of Iaguzhinsky who seemed to indicate that his mind had not yet been made up as far as John Deane was concerned. But the Factory and the chancellor were in accord. The Factory was Jacobite in essence and Iaguzhinsky supported their cause. They both hated John Deane and wanted him gone.

Eventually John Deane was instructed to present himself at the College of Foreign Affairs. At ten o'clock in the morning John Deane appeared before a panel consisting of Golovkin, Tolstoi, Stepanoff and another prominent Russian named Varsilley.

Golovkin spoke. Deane described Golvkin's tone as 'haughty'.

'Who sent you here?'

Deane replied that his 'own private affairs induced me to come,' but added that the king had approved his sending.

Golovkin wanted to know why the king would send Deane 'hither without any credentials'.

Deane said that he was not present in Russia as 'a public minister but as a consul to inspect into the grievance of trade'.

Deane was trying his best to rationalise the irrational, justifying why a man might arrive in a foreign country on an apparently self-appointed diplomatic mission that was somehow still approved of by the monarchy and the British government. It was a spirited defence but Golovkin wasn't interested in debating the point any further. He cut to the chase, choosing this moment to bring up Deane's chequered service record. He stated that Deane 'was an enemy to their country' who had 'committed faults while in their service' for which he had been 'sent into banishment'. Golovkin did not want such as Deane to stay in his homeland. The hammer had fallen. Once again John Deane was to be expelled from Russia.

Deane seemed to accept the decision very quickly. He turned his mind to practicalities.

'This is no time or place for me to justify myself,' he said. 'And since you force me away, please allow me know how many days will be allowed to give into the hand of some friends?'

Stepanoff told John Deane that he had a week to put his affairs in order. Deane was instructed to return the next day to receive his passport.

Deane would learn later that Tolstoi had spoken up for him. But the fact that the count had 'received and admitted' the Englishman had caused him some difficulty among his peers. Tolstoi's advocacy was appreciated but ultimately futile; the Jacobite/Holstein alliance had been too persuasive. Once details of John Deane's court martial had been requested from Admiralty College, Deane's fate was effectively sealed. The logic among those potentially ambivalent about Deane appeared to be that if Peter the Great had exiled the Englishman then that was that, he was not welcome in Russia.

John Deane returned to the College of Foreign Affairs to get his passport. He was made to wait several hours for Count Golovkin to come out of the senate. When Golovkin arrived, Deane was subject to another barrage of questions.

When Deane left for good, did he intend to 'travel by land or sea?'

Deane had 'not yet determined' his mode of transportation.

Golovkin and the attendant panel demanded that Deane be specific.

Deane refused to answer their question. Deane had very little in the way of retaliatory sticks with which to beat his enemies but this was one. His adversaries had had their way. They had defeated Deane's designs before they had ever properly got under way. What difference did it make how he left the country so long as he did it in the time prescribed? His refusal to answer the question annoyed his enemies disproportionately and Deane seemed to take a great deal of pleasure in their blustering and harrumphing. Nevertheless, many of Deane's enemies rejoiced rather conspicuously at his downfall. Iaguzhinsky and three members of the Factory went into the countryside and hurled themselves into a four-day eating and drinking binge in celebration of John Deane's defeat.

The next day John Deane received his passport. The passport gave Deane, 'liberty to travel by land or water'. He now had ten days to leave St Petersburg and one month to get out of Russia. The humiliation of Deane's return to Russia could only have been compounded by the brevity of his stay. But in the remaining time allotted to the English captain, John Deane met a man who promised to redeem the entire sorry business.

13

O'Connor

ritain was not completely blind in Russia and John
Deane was not entirely without friends in St Petersburg.
There was Joseph Ney with whom Deane lodged.
Information regarding Deane's support in the events leading up to
his expulsion had been leaked to him by an unnamed cabinet secretary. Dr Thomas Consett was a chaplain within the Factory. His
pro-Hanoverian stance and support of bishops in favour of friendly
relations with Britain had earned him overt persecution from
Factory members who spat at him and threatened to beat him with
their canes.

John Deane recruited informers while he was at St Petersburg.
There was an anonymous Factory member. There was Mr Trescod, a
former sailor-turned-landlord. Deane placed a high value on Trescod's
usefulness and friendship. Trescod spoke numerous languages. He
was very familiar 'with the state of maritime affairs' and in his position as publican associated with 'all men except those of a very high
degree'. Trescod intended to send his son to school in England. John
Deane hoped to assist him in placing the boy in a good school as a
reward for the exemplary service Trescod had provided in channelling
information to Deane. It was through Trescod that John Deane was
introduced to a young Irishman named Edmund O'Connor.

Two days before John Deane came to Kronslot, Edmund O'Connor
had attended a dinner at a general's house. The dinner was a Jacobite
gathering. Many of those present were discussing Deane's imminent arrival. The levels of venom directed at John Deane surprised
O'Connor and somewhat piqued his interest. 'I never knew a man
so hated and ill spoken of as he was this day at the general's table,'

O'Connor observed. Once John Deane arrived in Russia it was O'Connor's express intention to meet the reviled English captain.

Edmund O'Connor was a Jacobite. He was about 30 years old. He was cousin to Peter Lacey, a Jacobite general in the Russian army. O'Connor was a courier. Five months prior to Deane's arrival O'Connor had come to Russia from Spain. He had brought dispatches with him, which he delivered to prominent Jacobites. But O'Connor was disillusioned with the cause and wanted to leave. He was weary of Russia. He had sought a commission in the Russian army and had been offered a lieutenancy. He was insulted by the low rank and consequently resentful toward Russia. But mostly he was homesick and lovesick. He wanted to return to Ireland and settle down permanently in his country of origin where his fiancée waited for him.

For once, John Deane's appalling reputation abroad worked in his favour. O'Connor knew that Deane was in St Petersburg. He knew who John Deane was and everything negative he represented to the Jacobite cause in Russia. Through Trescod, O'Connor brokered a secret meeting with Deane and put his case to the Englishman. He wanted a pardon from the king of England. Deane told O'Connor that he could not authorise summary royal pardons but that he would use his influence to try and secure one on the Irishman's behalf. But O'Connor would have to earn his pardon. The condition was that O'Connor offer up information on his former compatriots. This was something O'Connor was perfectly willing to do and had already done in the early stages of his conversation with Deane.

Deane was particularly interested in a Scotsman named William Hay. Hay had been a captain in Peter the Great's navy. He had been dismissed from the Russian navy on his own request shortly after Deane's first expulsion. Deane knew William Hay and hated him. Hay was a Jacobite and his brother was a surgeon in the family of James III. Hay had been absent from Russia for two years. He had spent a considerable portion of that time in France, Italy and Spain. But about two weeks before Deane arrived in Russia William Hay returned and was currently staying with another prominent Jacobite named Henry Stirling.

Since setting foot in Russia, Deane had been convinced the Jacobites were planning something significant. Deane's suspicions were well-timed, aligning themselves with rumours in England that a dozen Russian ships were making ready to sail. Deane remembered the three men-of-war en route to Spain that he had seen on his journey to Kronslot. Stephen Poyntz, Townsend's man in Stockholm, had reported the movements of two known Jacobites. Poyntz believed the activity of the two Jacobites was linked to the destination and purpose of the three warships. Poyntz would go even further and claim that the three ships were carrying weapons and that the weapons had been deposited in Northern Scotland. Back in Britain, the alarmists in Walpole's government assumed that the combined weight of rumour pointed to one thing, a coordinated plan of invasion between Russia, Spain and Sweden designed to put James III back on the English throne. More cautious heads prevailed and Britain elected not to respond until more solid evidence was available.

John Deane assumed that William Hay was involved in whatever Jacobite plot was being devised. Prior to meeting O'Connor, Deane had tried unsuccessfully to 'learn Hay's business'. O'Connor was now perfectly placed to glean that information. Deane decided to take a chance on O'Connor. It was dangerous for O'Connor to risk being spotted with Captain Deane, so most of their communication was done through a trusted intermediary. Once a system of communication had been established, Deane schooled the Irishman on how to best position himself among his brethren to be of maximum usefulness. The first thing O'Connor needed to do was convince the Jacobites that he intended to return to Spain. Deane hoped that the Jacobites would use O'Connor to transport sensitive correspondence back across Europe. If the Jacobites took the bait then John Deane would encourage O'Connor to try and time his departure as would best 'answer the design of being entrusted with those letters'.

Deane wanted O'Connor to fully embed himself into the social fabric of Jacobite life in St Petersburg. O'Connor must do as the other Jacobites did to further win their confidence. To quickly accomplish this, John Deane gave O'Connor an important piece of hard-won wisdom. There was no better shortcut to securing fellow Jacobite affection than to insult Deane behind his back. So if O'Connor was in the company of Jacobites and they started defaming Deane, Deane encouraged the Irishman to join in. When the time came to leave Russia, O'Connor would need to be issued with a passport. As he was a foreigner this would normally take a fairly long time and would cost O'Connor money. Deane told the Irishman to consult a mutual friend who could get him a passport in four days. Deane had also instructed the friend to 'advance O'Connor forty roubles on his departure.' All things being well, if the Jacobites took the bait and entrusted O'Connor with letters, then O'Connor was to go straight to Hamburg where Deane would read the letters and pass them on to Townsend. Deane gave O'Connor the name of a contact in Hamburg who would tell the Irishman what to do next.

O'Connor updated Deane on what he heard about William Hay and why he was back in Russia. He knew that Hay had given his host Henry Stirling new instructions. O'Connor believed that Stirling had been told to 'reside at the Russian court'. O'Connor had heard half morsels of conversation about 'twelve ships of war' that were 'to be bought in Russia for the use of the Pretender'. The money for the purchase was put up by the papacy and by Spain. O'Connor told Deane he would try and get more information but encouraged him that if that was not possible, what was missing would almost certainly be contained in the letters he intended to deliver to Deane. O'Connor funnelled more rumours about William Hay and other enemies to John Deane. Hay's official reason for buying Russian ships was as a representative of the Mississippi Company. Hay and Stirling had been at Kronslot shortly after Deane's departure and had visited most of the ships in harbour there. O'Connor told Deane that he believed Golovkin was to be sent to Stockholm as an envoy. O'Connor finally confirmed what Deane had long suspected, that the Jacobites had known he was coming to Russia and had elaborately prepared to frustrate him the moment he entered their territory.

Deane naturally had his doubts about O'Connor. Deane's enemies were not stupid. Deane had considered the fact that O'Connor might well be acting 'the double part' – spying on Deane for the Jacobites by pretending to betray the cause. But having weighed all the circumstances, Deane believed that O'Connor's overtures were genuine. What finally convinced Deane was the intense determination O'Connor had shown to return to Ireland and live there for the rest of his days.

The day before Deane was due to leave St Petersburg, O'Connor contacted him. He told Deane that William Hay was set to leave Russia ten days hence. Deane told O'Connor to time his own departure 'for at least fourteen days after'. But if Hay stayed then O'Connor was to leave ten or twelve days after Deane.

It was time to go. John Deane's luggage was eventually returned to him the day before he was due to leave.

14

That Violent Spirit Now Ceasing

ohn Deane left St Petersburg on 22 June in the early hours
of the morning. He paid a final visit to his old friend
Apraxin. Once again the two men drank coffee together
and talked. Their conversation was conducted in the presence of
Apraxin's secretaries. Both men lamented the role the Factory had
played in evicting Deane from Russia. They mutually acknowledged
the sad truth that the Factory could not have operated with such
impunity without Russian patronage.

The conversation had been relatively formal and looked like it
had drawn to a close. John Deane rose to leave. Apraxin stopped
him. He asked Deane if he had anything he wished to say to him
alone, at which the Admiral's secretaries withdrew from the room.
John Deane spoke for a while, justifying his conduct in Russia.
He placed immense weight on the Factory's attempts to blacken
his name by invoking his court martial as the significant element
in his defeat. Apraxin expressed regret that Deane's past had been
used in such a manner. He reassured Deane that had he been present
in St Petersburg he would have 'endeavoured to prevent it'. Apraxin
believed that what had transpired over the last few weeks would not
damage Deane's reputation back home.

'You have the dismission that I gave you?' Apraxin asked.

'Yes,' Deane replied.

Deane told Apraxin that the 'dismission' to which the admiral referred, the papers that the admiral had given him when Peter

the Great had expelled him from Russia, had been shown to both Viscount Townsend and the king himself.

'Well then, they will certainly believe me to be as good a judge of you as an officer, as any that shall write against you.'

Apraxin asked Deane if he could do anything for him.

Deane asked Apraxin to think well of George I and take Townsend's message as sincere. He wished for Apraxin to 'continue his kindness' to the king and 'not easily credit' Jacobite rumours that over-exaggerated their support in Great Britain. Deane reassured Apraxin that 'everything was entirely easy and calm in Great Britain,' but admitted that as far as a minor Jacobite presence in his country was concerned, 'the spirit of that party was never quite distinguished'.

Apraxin stood up. He told Deane that he would be England's friend in working towards reconciliation. Apraxin ended the conversation on a note of warning. He seemed to classify himself as part of an older, nobler stock of Russian that prized peace with Great Britain, but he cautioned Deane that 'there are younger men that have different ways of thinking'. Apraxin saluted Deane and the two men parted company.

John Deane left Kronslot on 23 June. Aboard the ship were two friends of Deane's, Captain Commodore Lane and Richard Brown, the master builder who had turned Deane's beloved *Samson* into such a formidable warship. John Deane also shared passage with certain officers who he believed had come aboard 'chiefly to satisfy their curiosity' about him 'and to make observations'; men Deane suspected 'should be very glad to accompany me out of Russia'.

John Deane was headed for Stockholm to inform Stephen Poyntz of 'the state of affairs'. He continued his journey by boat and was put ashore at Gothland on 5 July. Deane ordered that his baggage be delivered to a Mr Tighe. Deane rode to Wisby looking for a vessel that could transport him to Stockholm. His travelling alias was that of a merchant. Deane needed to move quickly but couldn't find any commercial vessel that wasn't departing 'in several days' time'. The only swift option was to try and persuade a fishing boat to take him onboard. No fisherman would transport him so long as he was alone and pretending to be a merchant. They would transport him if he could drum up a few more paying passengers to make it worth their while. Deane tried and failed. He dropped the pretence of being a merchant and 'declared himself a seaman'. One of the fishing boats welcomed him aboard. Deane left Wisby on 8 July and was set ashore at Aiver two days later. It took two more boat journeys to get him to Stockholm. He met Poyntz where he was given travel documents for the rest of the journey. Deane wrote to his confidantes in Russia instructing them to send a messenger to Poyntz in the event of an emergency.

Deane arrived in Hamburg on 19 July. He left instructions with the man he had ordered to meet O'Connor to look after the Irishman when he eventually arrived. Deane sat down and wrote a letter to O'Connor reassuring him that he would do everything in his capacity to secure the pardon the Irishman craved. John Deane left Hamburg and travelled on to Hanover. He arrived in Hanover on 19 July.

Deane wrote his account of the short brutal tenure in Kronslot and St Petersburg. He charted the twists and turns of his adventures with Apraxin, Golovkin, O'Connor and the Factory. But Deane also included his observations on the state of Russia under Catherine I. It seemed a vastly different country from the one he had served not that long ago. It was a more dissolute place than he remembered and seemed even more subject to factions than it had been under the tsar. The new Russia was a place afflicted by a strange inertia and a sense of rapid decay. Yet despite this, Russia was drunk on confidence. Deane believed that this had more to do with foreign perceptions of Russian strength than the sad reality of the state of their navy. The three ships that Deane had observed in Elsinor had caused panic among the Danes. At dinner with Apraxin, John Deane had witnessed Prince Menishikoff launch into a ruthless broadside at the king of Denmark's expense for being so frightened of the three Russian ships that he had forced his own people to work on the Sabbath in preparation for an anticipated Russian onslaught.

Deane included his own and others' observations about the double-faced nature of the grief shown to the dead tsar in his report. Deane predicted that once 'the mourning is over, both the Empress, as well as this court, will launch into all manner of gaiety, luxury and effeminacy'. Deane reported that Admiral Sievers had told him of the relief among 'the senate and other Russians of family' now that Peter the Great was dead, because of 'the continental hurry the late tsar kept them in'. Yet, despite himself, John Deane seemed to lament the lost industry and brilliance of the tsar. Deane's report contained a half sentence that read like a bitter epigrammatic eulogy for the fallen ruler, his achievements and their ephemeral nature: 'that violent spirit now ceasing, those things, that were all forced, will in a little while also cease'.

15

Tell Me What You Will Undertake And I Will Do It

When the intelligence Deane had gathered reached Townsend and the more alarmist members of Walpole's government, Deane's reports of the three ships, then the twelve ships, William Hay, proposed Spanish and papal plots, and the possibility of a Jacobite invasion, placed him in a valued position on the continent. What should have been a disaster had worked out exceptionally well for John Deane. He had been an appalling diplomat; how could anybody with John Deane's genius for making committed, impassioned and spiteful enemies have been anything otherwise? But Deane had proved himself an outstanding spy. Out of the wreckage of his time at St Petersburg he had managed to recruit an informer so valuable that an actual invasion might be averted if O'Connor was handled correctly. John Deane had a new vocation.

It was August and plans had changed. O'Connor was to be sent to Amsterdam rather than Hamburg. He had succeeded in convincing the Jacobites in Russia to employ him as a courier. He had agreed to take Jacobite dispatches to France and Spain but had arranged to go straight to Amsterdam. Townsend had ordered John Deane to meet O'Connor there. Deane was keen to get to Amsterdam before O'Connor and arrived there at midnight.

Townsend was in Hanover with the king. Townsend was not fully convinced about O'Connor. He did not share Deane's full confidence in the Irishman, and he had not yet decided whether he was going to use O'Connor. As a precautionary measure he ordered Deane to 'penetrate into his designs and prevent him making ill use of anything, should he be a Jacobin'. Deane and Townsend would correspond through written dispatch, with Deane keeping Townsend informed of every shift in the O'Connor business. Townsend would give great weight to Deane's opinions but the viscount would ultimately have the last word in how, or if, O'Connor would be put to work.

O'Connor had not yet arrived but had sent advanced word to Deane. O'Connor had arranged that 'all letters for him might be taken in to' Deane. There were three letters sent in advance of O'Connor that the Irishman had offered as a sign of good faith. Deane intended to copy the letters, retain the originals and send the duplicates to Townsend. But a little of Townsend's reticence seemed to have rubbed off on Deane. Deane made preparations to intercept O'Connor the moment he arrived, 'from the first minute in order to prevent him disposing of any letter without letting me have a sight of them'. He wrote to Townsend stating: 'I shall keep both the man and original letters till I receive your Lordships' further command.'

The three letters were from Henry Stirling, Admiral Gordon and Captain Hay. The letters contained a reference to £20,000 and mentions of 'a certain man' who had been 'very busy in the Rebellion of 1718', who for the past seven years had been going backwards and forwards from Russia to England. Although the man was not named, Deane believed he knew him. He was a Jabobite of whom Deane had always harboured suspicions. Deane wrote to Townsend requesting that the man be arrested at Gravesend, detained and examined. As far as O'Connor's credibility was concerned, the three letters were a promising down payment.

Eventually O'Connor arrived in Amsterdam with more letters. O'Connor was ready to be put to work. But almost as soon as he had come to Amsterdam, a letter arrived from Dr Consett, Deane's friend in St Petersburg. The letter had been written in a hurry and warned of a possible problem with O'Connor. A woman had approached the Jacobite General Peter Lacey and had denounced O'Connor as a traitor. The woman had an immoral reputation and Lacey refused to believe anything scandalous she had to say about his cousin.

A drunken indiscretion nearly destroyed Edmund O'Connor's career as a spy when he spoke in his sleep to a lady of dubious virtue. *Illustration by Stephen Dennis*

John Deane pressed O'Connor as to how this situation might have come about. O'Connor, who had previously ascribed his motives for betraying the Jacobite cause as being rooted in the love of a good woman, admitted that he had got drunk and had sex with the lady in question. In those post-coital moments, half asleep and half awake, he had said something incriminating. Deane was mortified and somewhat embarrassed. He wrote to Townsend justifying his choice of O'Connor, insisting that he had properly vetted him in relation to his sobriety and that 'no man is more cautious of transacting affairs with men that are drunk than I am'.

John Deane detained O'Connor for eight days while he waited for instructions from Townsend as to what to do next. O'Connor tried to make himself useful and copied out Jacobite letters that Deane forwarded to Townsend. In that time, O'Connor talked extensively with Deane. He advertised his indispensability, dropping the names of members of the Jacobite high command, stating that he was 'very well-known' by Gordon in Bordeaux and Archdeacon in Rotterdam, Jacobites for whom he had letters. He offered to go and see Archdeacon to deliver his letters in person. He assured Deane that he could get more information out of Archdeacon that way. He then proposed to go to Bordeaux, Spain and then on to Ireland if Townsend would permit him, gathering information en route. He had even heard that the Jacobites had an extensive cache of weapons hidden in Ireland. He would return and relay everything he had learned to Townsend and Deane.

John Deane was quite taken with the proposal. Deane was particularly interested in a name in one the letters in O'Connor's dispatch addressed to Peter Lacey. The name was O'Donovon, an extremely well-connected Jacobite currently resident in the west of Ireland. O'Connor was friends with O'Donovon and perfectly willing to betray him.

O'Connor was winning Deane's confidence back after the inebriated sexual indiscretion in Russia. Deane was excited about the possible damage O'Connor might do to the Jacobites and was happy to promote O'Connor's cavalier proposal if it meant hurting their cause. In his letter to Townsend, Deane championed O'Connor afresh, mentioning that the Irishman had expressed a desire to convert from Catholicism to Protestantism. For O'Connor's part, if he was going back to Ireland, and if he was going to betray his countrymen and close friends risking his life in the process, he needed a royal pardon. If that was not possible, he required some form of official diplomatic documentation from Townsend that might deflect the possibility of retaliatory violence if he were to be caught.

Townsend quickly put aside his initial misgivings about O'Connor. The Viscount was as taken with O'Connor's bold proposition as Deane was and gave Deane permission to 'dispatch him as soon as possible with his letters'. Townsend approved the pardon. He sent a courier to Deane with £100 for O'Connor. John Deane was to be keeper of the purse. Townsend gave Deane full authority to control the flow of money as he saw fit. Townsend was keen for O'Connor to get going as soon as possible. He suggested a contingency plan if O'Connor's true purpose was discovered by their enemies before the Irishman left them. Deane was to give O'Connor a reward and his pardon, and then O'Connor was to go to ground for five or six months. Townsend emphasised to Deane the importance of thoroughly interviewing O'Connor on his return from Spain and Ireland, and milking every drop of information he could provide from the Jacobite heartlands.

It was September. October was agreed as the best time for O'Connor to begin his journey. Townsend sent a further £100. The viscount tried to pre-empt anything that might go wrong with O'Connor's mission. He recommended Mr Stanhope, the English ambassador in Madrid, as a trusted man to whom O'Connor could deliver his intelligence if it was too dangerous to return to Deane. Townsend was concerned about O'Connor carrying large amounts of money across Europe. Townsend suggested that Deane give half the allotted money to the Irishman. Then Townsend instructed Deane to take a playing card, cut it in half and give it to O'Connor. The other half of the card and the rest of the money was to be taken to Townsend who would forward card and money to Stanhope in Spain. When O'Connor arrived in Spain, whoever approached him with the other half of the card could be trusted and would give the Irishman the rest of his money. Townsend was keen to establish correspondence between Deane and Stanhope. Townsend's attention turned to O'Connor in Ireland. The Viscount was particularly interested in the weapons O'Connor had referred to. Townsend wanted to know where they were. He wanted them seized and would remunerate O'Connor generously if he could discover their whereabouts. Townsend suggested a £500 reward. Come October, John Deane sent Edmund O'Connor on the first stage of his journey. He was to go to Rotterdam and see Archdeacon. Things progressed without suspicion on the part of the Jacobite. O'Connor delivered letters to Archdeacon and was given letters for O'Connor to take back to William Hay. O'Connor copied the letters and sent them to Deane in Amsterdam.

Townsend received news from Spain that disturbed him. An ally had been taken in his bed by the Spanish authorities who had forced their way into his room and imprisoned him in a castle in Granada. In the light of this news, sending O'Connor to Spain now seemed disproportionately risky to the viscount. Townsend sent Deane alternate orders regarding the Irishman. He wanted Deane to instruct O'Connor to 'skulk about in Holland or any other place' and for the Irishman to 'settle a correspondence with you that you may always know how to write to him'. O'Connor was effectively being put on ice until Townsend could figure out how best to use him without unnecessarily endangering his life. O'Connor had not yet received his pardon. The pardon had been approved. Townsend had the document with him and was anxious to pass it on to the Irishman. All he needed to know was how to correctly spell the Irishman's Christian name.

O'Connor had been busy in Rotterdam. There was a lot of confused activity. O'Connor tried his best to keep Deane informed. An unnamed man from France had arrived with a letter for 'their man at Rotterdam'. O'Connor told Deane, who then instructed O'Connor to get the messenger drunk and get him talking. There was a letter from Gordon. There was an Irish clerk present whom O'Connor knew. O'Connor obtained a handwriting sample of Archdeacon's French clerk and a sample of Archdeacon's seal. O'Connor discovered the route the correspondence between Archdeacon and his friends in Russia would take. The Irishman was doing very well but was conscious of outstaying his welcome and arousing Archdeacon's suspicion. Nevertheless, Deane instructed him to stay where he was and further win Archdeacon's confidence.

O'Connor did as ordered. Deane's instincts proved correct. Archdeacon seemed quite taken with O'Connor and asked the Irishman if he would accompany him to Spain. Deane was excited. He did not yet know that Townsend was losing confidence in the Spanish venture. Deane wrote to Townsend approving the arrangement the viscount had made with Stanhope. Deane had faith in O'Connor and the Spanish mission. In contrast with Townsend, Deane's approach to the possibility of failure in Spain was to prepare O'Connor to succeed somewhere else. O'Connor was in correspondence with William Hay. Deane encouraged the Irishman to 'flatter' Hay 'and desire he would mention his name to his brothers'. William Hay's brothers lived in Italy. Deane was guiding O'Connor to pave the way to be of use in Italy if things in Spain did not go well.

O'Connor observed more comings and goings in Rotterdam. There was another anonymous man who came to see Archdeacon. The stranger was from the north of England; tall, between 20 and 30 years old, level-headed and reticent.

O'Connor had eight days before he was due to travel to Spain and there was much to accomplish before he departed. There was a clan of Jacobites who flocked around a lieutenant. The lieutenant was either Spanish or Italian and carried a heavily locked leather bag with him. The lieutenant and his cronies were notably excited about something O'Connor had not yet discovered. O'Connor had befriended the lieutenant and was to drink tea with him. Deane instructed O'Connor to go one step further and take the lieutenant round Rotterdam: 'Show him some rarity, separate him from the clan and then "attack him with the bottle".' The last visceral instruction was John Deane's exquisite euphemism for getting a victim hammered on alcohol and encouraging him to talk, a favourite technique of Deane's for extracting sensitive information.

Deane received the dispatch from Townsend effectively aborting the Spanish mission. O'Connor's trip to Ireland also seemed to be in question. Deane was stunned. He sent a reply respectfully imploring Townsend to change his mind. Deane stressed the time. He believed that such an opportunity might not present itself to O'Connor again. He even offered to accompany O'Connor on the Ireland chapter of his journey if that would help. Deane gave the letter to O'Connor. He ordered O'Connor to deliver the letter to Townsend in person. Deane hoped that the Irishman's presence, earnestness and enthusiasm would sway things. Deane sent O'Connor on his way him giving a new name to travel under: William Wilson.

Deane seemed beset by worries. He had received word from St Petersburg that Dr Consett was suffering persecutions at the hands of the Jacobites. Deane's promise to educate the son of the publican Trescod was weighing on him. Deane asked Townsend if he could help in any way in either situation. 'It has never been my method to neglect my absent friends,' he told Townsend. Deane had also been thinking about his own future. The business with O'Connor was exciting and important but in financial terms it was only an adjunct to his responsibilities in St Petersburg and would, one way or the other, soon be over, then once again John Deane would be unemployed. John Deane was worrying about ageing. He had already written to Townsend and diplomatically asked for work, or else a pension, 'to move beyond the dreadful apprehension of want in old age'.

Deane waited for O'Connor to return. He wrote two letters to Townsend. Deane was determined to get his way in the matter of O'Connor and Spain. Punctuating the letter with more of the obsequious praise he was wont to include in his correspondence with Townsend, Deane offered further suggestions as to how to make O'Connor's mission a possibility. Once again he politely asked for further work once his part in the O'Connor business had run its course.

O'Connor and Townsend met. Townsend liked the Irishman. He found O'Connor, 'plain in what he says and does not pretend to more knowledge of things than he really has'. As Townsend talked to O'Connor he learned that while the Irishman certainly moved in exalted Jacobite circles he was never taken into the heart of Jacobite confidence, was never told the designs of the letters he was carrying or was 'employed in the manner of any intrigues'. But O'Connor and Townsend's conversation led to a misunderstanding that perplexed O'Connor somewhat. Townsend had either disregarded, or hadn't received John Deane's assessment that O'Connor wanted to convert from Catholicism to Protestantism. Townsend talked to the Irishman, 'as supposing him a rigid papist', prompting Deane to reassure Townsend that, 'I find his aversion to superstition had been of some standing and have provided him with some books of divinity'.

Despite seeing O'Connor for himself, Townsend was still opposed to sending him to Spain where the Irishman might be in danger, or else expose the breach in Jacobite intelligence. Townsend was not completely hostile to the idea of using O'Connor in Ireland. But the viscount would not hastily commit to an Irish adventure. 'It may be managed as well a month or two hence as now,' he would tell Deane. Townsend felt that once he had returned to England he would be in a better position to oversee a safer entry into Ireland for O'Connor.

Townsend sent O'Connor back to Deane. Deane was to make sure O'Connor passed his time there without raising suspicion. Both men were to keep their eyes and ears open and gather intelligence. Deane was to create a system of communication with O'Connor in the event that O'Connor be sent anywhere on Jacobite business. They were to do this until Townsend left Hanover. Townsend had O'Connor's pardon. He didn't give it to O'Connor but sent it separately to John Deane to keep. Townsend's logic was that 'it would be wrong he should have such a paper on him, till it is time for him to make up of it'.

Considering his exalted position in the British government and place on the European stage, and also considering how much he feared and hated the Jacobites, Townsend was surprisingly squeamish about the possibility of genuine harm coming to O'Connor in pursuit of a mission that could have seriously damaged Jacobite efforts. John Deane was far less concerned about sending Edmund O'Connor into the heart of the lion's den. Deane was a soldier who had carried out and issued orders that had resulted in the loss of men's lives. Townsend wasn't. Deane had known hardship and seen death in many of its cruel manifestations. Lest it ever be forgot, he had eaten human flesh to stay alive. John Deane was clearly more comfortable with hard decisions of this nature. He was certainly more comfortable with sending O'Connor into situations that might result in his capture, torture or execution than Townsend appeared to be. But Deane also seemed to take O'Connor's boldness at face value. He respected it. After all, it was O'Connor who had encouraged the Spanish venture in the first place. He wanted to do it, and if he was successful, the rewards for the Irishman would be astronomical. Deane clearly liked O'Connor. There was something oddly paternal in the way Deane schooled O'Connor in the ways of Georgian espionage. The two men copied and forged letters together and Deane told Townsend of how O'Connor would insist on 'my transcribing some paragraph which I had read to him of your Lordship's letter'. The 'paragraph' was presumably the viscount's handwritten reassurances of O'Connor's clemency; a comforting mantra for the Irishman. Like a father Deane tried to 'instil frugality and caution' into O'Connor. On the subject of money, Deane was not in complete agreement with Townsend's doctrine of generosity towards the Irishman. Deane advised against giving O'Connor too much money, as the Irishman's reputation among his friends and family was that of being perpetually broke. There was also a practical logic to withholding funds from O'Connor: 'It will keep him more dependent and less exposed to temptation.' O'Connor, for all his good intentions, had a hedonistic streak in him. But John Deane's ultimate pronouncement on Edmund O'Connor was that he was 'not without notions of honour, gratitude and generosity'. This was most evident in an oft repeated refrain O'Connor would offer up to Deane: 'Tell me what you will undertake and I will do it.'

Deane wanted O'Connor to be active. He felt that keeping him hidden was counterproductive. Deane wanted to send O'Connor among the Jacobites in Bruges or Bordeaux where he might re-establish his credibility and gather intelligence that could illuminate what was being planned in Spain and Ireland. But O'Connor and Deane's time together was almost at an end. The rest of October was a flurry of activity that promised a great deal but ultimately didn't really amount to very much. Deane travelled to The Hague to see Townsend. Golovkin was spotted in a nearby town before sailing to Germany. Suspicious people came and went in Rotterdam and Amsterdam, all observed and reported by Deane and O'Connor. Deane got an associate of Archdeacon's drunk and wheedled information out of him about Jacobite movements to Spain, still something of an obsession with Deane. All the time John Deane itched to take O'Connor off his leash and let him accompany some such group of promising Jacobites or another to some incriminating destination. But Deane was under perpetual constraint by Townsend; forbidden from using O'Connor as he thought best. Yet Deane's relationship with Townsend and respect for his judgement was good and the confidence was reciprocated. Although the O'Connor adventure had, chiefly because of Townsend's caution, yielded less than it had promised, the viscount was pleased enough with Deane to allay a deep-rooted fear in the English captain, that of unemployment and destitution. At last, Townsend offered Deane the prospect of future service. The good news elicited from Deane a paragraph of particularly obsequious thanks in a letter to his patron.

Deane received further news of Dr Consett's harsh treatment at the hands of the Factory in St Petersburg. Deane believed that Consett was suffering because of him, that Consett's support had earned the doctor his current persecutions. Deane had implored Townsend to help. He feared that without intervention Consett would be treated, 'as they have done to me, and make him blacker to the eyes of the unseeing multitude than ever Ethiopian was'. Townsend referred the matter to Walpole who agreed to intercede on Consett's behalf. But with relations between Britain and Russia so antagonistic, even Walpole's intervention was limited in what it could accomplish and seemed to amount to very little. Dr Consett would leave Russia in 1727, effectively hounded out of the country. But Townsend had tried, and that carried weight with John Deane, further cementing his loyalty to the viscount.

It was November and the final days of John Deane's time with O'Connor were spent moving between Amsterdam and Rotterdam managing the Irishman and investigating rumours that Captain William Hay had been seen moving among the local Jacobite community. Descriptions of the man believed to be Hay had been sent to Townsend from an agent in Berlin. Townsend had passed the description on to Deane. As far as Deane was concerned, the man could not be Hay because the height was wrong and the Jacobite's face had not been commented upon in the report. If the man was truly Hay then the Berliner could not have resisted mentioning his 'long visage' or 'large teeth much exposed to view either in a laugh or a smile'. It could not be Hay because Hay had a black servant that the Berliner would also have commented upon. Also, the livery of the servant was green, a faux pas for anybody who spent as much time in Russia as

Hay did. 'It would not be well to give it green in Russia, neither can I believe he would do it abroad,' Deane reported. The man believed to be Hay had spoken in an Irish accent. This appeared to have been interpreted as a 'put on' accent by the Berliner. Deane rubbished this idea. Hay was Scottish and too proud of being a Scot to ever pass himself off as Irish, even for the purpose of establishing cover. Deane did not believe Hay had been in the vicinity. Deane's old enemy Golovkin was now in Stockholm. Hay and Golovkin were close friends who had served together in the armed forces. If Townsend really wanted to know where Hay was likely to be then he should look to Sweden and Golovkin.

On one level, Deane's report to Townsend was yet another example of the kind of shaggy dog episodes that typified his final moments in Amsterdam. But it was interesting in that it revealed Deane's concise and astute powers of recall and observation, his ability to interpret a situation, his skill as an intelligence officer and ultimately his indispensability to Townsend.

16

Neither at Peace or at War

ate November 1725 was quiet. Deane's last letter to Townsend that month was a letter apologising for not having sent a letter recently because nothing had happened. In its early stages the O'Connor business promised to birth one of the great tales of the pioneering days of espionage, but in the end appeared to amount to very little. Yet it was deceptive to think of it like that. O'Connor's recruitment and the information he had provided was vital. He had confirmed what Townsend had feared, that Jacobites were embedded across Europe. Townsend now knew that they were well-funded, organised and supported by many of Britain's enemies. He realised that they were particularly entrenched in the Russian court and posed an authentic threat to Hanoverian stability. Thanks to Deane and O'Connor, Townsend knew the identities and character of much of the Jacobite high command. In O'Connor they still had a man on the inside if they could ever decide on how further to use him. From Townsend's point of view, O'Connor's role had been vital in confirming that the Jacobites had been talking about the utilisation of twelve Russian ships paid for by Spain and the papacy. Combined with existing intelligence and Deane's first-hand knowledge of the three ships bound for Spain, Townsend was convinced an invasion was imminent. The fact that O'Connor was reporting a half-heard conversation and that Deane had decried the three ships as 'good for nothing' did not arrest Townsend's determination to prepare for the worst. New intelligence that seemed to suggest that the Russian navy in Revel was preparing for war could only confirm Townsend's deepest suspicions. Townsend was now fully convinced that a Russian/Spanish coalition supporting the Jacobites would invade Scotland and the west of England simultaneously. Townsend believed the invasion was six months away. Townsend lobbied for certain Russian ships to be seized and searched. He wanted an increased show of naval strength in the West Indies where it was believed money was being sent to fund the Jacobite rebels. Walpole intervened.

Although initially cynical about the levels of Jacobite organisation, the prime minister soon changed his mind. Walpole seemed to have a better understanding than his foreign secretary of the military resources available to Britain and the need to tread carefully with other nations. To send the British navy to the West Indies was too provocative. It would also spread the navy out too thinly when they would be better employed near their own coast in strength. Walpole split the navy into two fleets. One fleet would patrol the British coast. The other would patrol the Baltic. It was a pre-emptive exercise in muscle flexing designed to avoid a war if at all possible. All the while Townsend was free to hunt for weapons in Scotland and try to get to the bottom of what the three Russian ships were doing in Spain.

Deane and O'Connor's time together was at an end. They went their separate ways. O'Connor received his pardon and a £100 reward for services to the Crown. Deane wrote up his account of his time in Russia in an official document entitled *An Account of Affairs in Russia, June–July 1725*. He also wrote an intelligence report entitled *The Present State of the Maritime Power of Russia*. Townsend made good on his promise and secured Deane a position. With the increase of British warships in the Baltic, Captain John Deane had been ordered to accompany Sir Charles Wagner's squadron as both a political adviser and an interpreter. At least those were his official orders. In reality, Townsend had sent Deane on another spying mission. Deane was to scour the coast, seeking out sympathetic acquaintances and old friends whose friendly conversation he might convert into intelligence and information that shed further light on Russia's intentions and Jacobite movements.

John Deane spent the spring and summer of 1726 stationed on board the *Torbay*, a 540-man, 80-gun warship, making forays into the coastal ports as and when opportunity dictated.

Writing in April to Townsend from Copenhagen, John Deane mentioned that he had dined with a Russian named Mr Beltashoff. The dinner was ostensibly friendly but Deane knew that he was being gleaned for information about the strength and destination of the British squadron and how long they were likely to remain in the area. Deane was sociable. He gave nothing away but sought to extract his own information from Beltashoff who appeared to have news regarding a trio of Russian ships. Some time previously, three Russian ships had passed by that way from Spain. According to Beltashoff the ships' cargo had been, 'oil and wine, and some fruit that they had taken in at Cadiz'. The ships had been forced to winter in Spain. The perishable part of their cargo had rotted. Beltashoff informed Deane that the presence of the three ships in Cadiz was a mercantile statement of intent from Russia. Their presence in Cadiz was intended to show that Russian ships were now fit to engage in trade in the East Indies and Madagascar, although the Russians had not yet secured any trade treaties in those provinces.

Beltashoff was disturbed at the presence of so many British warships so far north when he believed 'we and all the powers this way were at peace'. In reply, Deane invoked his conversation with Count Tostoi. He informed Beltashoff that relations between Russia and England existed in a strange martial limbo where both nations were 'neither at peace or at war'. Deane wanted to know about recent Russian demonstrations of naval strength. Beltashoff said that any show of strength was a false display of power. The Russians were keen to appear more 'formidable than they really are'. Beltashoff estimated the present strength of the Russian navy to have been little more than 'twelve ships of the line and two or three frigates' that were fit to sail.

In May, John Deane went to Stockholm and spoke with a baron whom he had served in Russia. The baron had information 'related to the Russians' preparations'. Walpole's strategy appeared to be effective. The Russians had not expected the British fleet to appear on their doorstep. The good news was tempered with bad. The baron relayed information regarding old friends and enemies. Apraxin was 'rather desirous of retiring than commanding at sea'. As far as his replacement was concerned it seemed unlikely that Deane's ally Sievers would be given command of the fleet as he did not have the confidence of the Russian court. Deane's old foe Thomas Gordon was most likely to succeed Apraxin, should he retire.

In late May the British squadron arrived at Revel. The Russians were thrown into a state of panic, believing that they were about to be attacked.

In the hunt for information, John Deane lost a contact and gained a contact. Gustaf Armfelt, a Swedish general Deane had arranged to speak to effectively stood him up. Instead Deane sought out a prominent person he described as a 'good king's man' who supported Hanoverian interests. Deane spent a night and a morning with his new associate trying to convince him to offer up any information that might be useful to British interests in the area. Deane's prospective informer was 'not unwilling but shy on the hazard should it be known'. Still, the intelligence gleaned was encouraging. The king's man told Deane of 'two couriers' who had passed by recently and a 'Russian count' who 'was in great consternation' of the British presence in the Baltic. The count endeavoured 'to put everything in a posture of defence at Kronslot', having received 'intelligence from England' that the British intended to assault the port.

The king's man was in weekly correspondence with an aristocrat in St Petersburg from whom he obtained useful information. Relaying intelligence would prove awkward. The king's man was willing to pass information on to Deane but did not want to commit anything to writing. He would only tell Deane what he had discovered face to face, so that Deane had to contrive a reason to leave his official duties and be ferried, on a weekly basis, to see his new informer personally.

In June 1726 Deane learned that overdue prize money for ships captured by the Russian navy between 1718 and 1719 in the Great Northern War was being paid out. Some of that money belonged to Deane. He was incensed. Despite the futility of his suite, Deane wanted his money. He wrote to Admiral Apraxin asking for his assistance in ensuring that any wages he had earned were somehow forwarded to him. Deane also wrote to Townsend imploring the viscount to intervene in the matter on his behalf.

Aboard the *Torbay*, moored in the waters of Revel, as the summer drew to a close John Deane came into close proximity with a truly despised old enemy.

Deane was highly valued by Admiral Wagner and was a welcome guest at his dinner table. He enjoyed dining with the admiral. For John Deane, dinner was a form of sanctuary from the intensity and sometime madness of his duties. He described the custom in intimate terms as a place where, 'we live here in tranquillity, not forgetting our friends in a glass after dinner'. The serpent in Eden was Thomas Saunders. The Jacobite admiral had been invited to dinner. As Russia and Britain were neither at peace nor war, diplomacy occasionally demanded that old enemies became temporary dinner guests. When Saunders came to dinner, the atmosphere appeared as one of strained politeness. One of Saunders favourite weapons was mockery. At the dinner table he sought to undermine John Deane with an observation. Deane recalled how Thomas Saunders compared 'me to mercury, by my quick removal from England to St Petersburg, Stockholm, Hanover, The Hague, England and now again in Revel'.

Having eaten on board Wagner's ship, Saunders was obliged to return the compliment. But that courtesy did not extend to John Deane, who was not invited to eat aboard Saunders' vessel. Yet Deane was the topic of conversation. Saunders talked for an hour about John Deane. He praised Townsend who he believed was 'a man of sense' but was incredulous that the viscount should put any kind of stock in John Deane's abilities. Saunders sent a personal message back to the *Torbay* for John Deane to contemplate. Deane had enjoyed a surprising degree of movement on the Russian mainland that summer. He had been ashore to Revel at least three times that season. Saunders issued a barely concealed threat. As far as he was concerned, Deane's liberty was now at an end. Saunders let it be known that 'it was not safe' for Deane 'to come any more on land'.

17

Revisions

John Deane returned to England. His duties in the Baltic almost at an end, Deane was once again facing the prospect of unemployment. Resident in London, having let it lie dormant for a decade and a half, Deane revisited his old Boon Island narrative. In autumn 1726 he published a revised account of the wreck of the *Nottingham Galley* entitled *A Narrative of the Nottingham Galley, &c, Published in 1711. Revis'd and re-printed with Additions in 1726, by John Deane, Commander.*

The revised edition told more or less the same story as his brother's version. The most notable stylistic difference was that now the narrative was told in the third person. There was no introduction. Deane leapt straight into the account. He fleshed out the narrative with more detail than Jasper Deane or Christopher Langman had included. He omitted any mention of French privateers or the attempted murder of the first mate. He told the story (missing from the Jasper Deane account) of the attempted theft of the extra ration of human flesh. He provided a coda (also omitted from the Jasper Deane account) where he described his arrival in New England and his haggard black comic encounter in the home of his rescuer Jethro Furber. As the hero of his own narrative, John Deane presented himself as a man blessed by God, 'in a greater share of health and strength of body, and likewise a proportionate vigour of mind', for the purpose of instilling 'into the hearts of the dispirited people a reliance on that almighty being, who is not confin'd to particular means, nor always acts to human probabilities'. In other words, Deane was the modest deliverer, appointed by his creator to lead his men to safety. Although no less dramatic in its storytelling, John Deane's account was generally a more reflective narrative than those that had preceded it. The reader had greater access to Deane's internal agonising over the impossible decisions he had been forced to make on a daily basis. Most importantly, it was a narrative stripped of the original agenda that had necessitated its predecessor. The crew, including Langman, were given their due in much the same way they had been in the Jasper Deane account. But gone was the sting in the tail, the defensive postscript fending off assaults on the Deane brothers' reputations. The closing paragraphs of the new account were conciliatory and seasoned with a degree of grace for old enemies. John Deane wrote: 'At the first publication of this narrative, the master, the mate and Mr Whitworth were all in England; but, in a course of fifteen years since, the master alone survives of all that he particularly knew.' With the perspective of time and from the privileged vantage point of survival, Deane could afford to be magnanimous. In the closing paragraph of his account he announced his intention to make provision for an 'annual commemoration of their wonderful deliverance' to be held in New England for 'those beneficent gentlemen, whose admir'd humanity on this occasion deserves applause and imitation throughout succeeding ages', as well as 'to prove of service to reclaim some of the unthinking part of his own fraternity'.

It was a noble and undoubtedly sincere sentiment but not without a possible dash of self-interest. John Deane could have initiated a memorial without the public hoo-ha of a fresh pamphlet opening old wounds. The Boon Island incident and its subsequent pamphlet war was after all the reason that John Deane had spent over a decade in self-imposed exile. But as well as being a survivor, John Deane was also a pragmatist. He was out of work. There was the immediate need for money and further employment. Up until now, publicity had mostly been John Deane's enemy. Now it could work in his favour. For the first time John Deane took ownership of his legacy. He wouldn't run from Boon Island anymore. He would take possession of it and make it work on his behalf. The pamphlet would bring in an immediate source of income. It sold well and was reprinted the following year. More importantly, it made Deane a public figure once again. It placed him back in the public's awareness while he sought a new appointment. And there was a post that John Deane was specifically interested in: the commercial consul for the ports of Flanders and Ostend was up for grabs. Walpole, Townsend and Sir Charles Wagner were all keen for John Deane to have the post. The renewed celebrity the pamphlet provided could help secure the post. Deane's strategy proved successful. He was offered the consulship.

The pamphlet revealed a tragic detail in John Deane's personal life. He wrote, 'At the first publication of this narrative, the master, the mate and Mr Whitworth, were all in England; but, in a course of fifteen years since, the master alone survives of all that he particularly knew'. As far as he was aware, John Deane was now the only surviving veteran of Boon Island. Among those that had passed away since John Deane had left England for Russia was his brother. Jasper Deane had died on 23 October 1723, aged 70 years. He was buried in St Wilfrid's church cemetery. His tombstone declared that he had been married four times and had fathered 'several children'.

Before John Deane was dispatched on his last great adventure, there was some unfinished business to attend to. Lord Townsend's obsession throughout Deane's tenure as interpreter and political adviser to Sir Charles Wagner had been the fear of an imminent Russian-funded Jacobite invasion of the British Isles. Townsend desperately wanted to get to the bottom of what the three Russian ships bound for Cadiz, the ships that Deane had originally spotted in Elsinore, had been up to. Townsend still believed that the purpose of the ships was to deliver weapons to the Irish and Scottish supporters of James III. Townsend's spies were busy all around Europe trying to pull together the different strands of the alleged conspiracy, or else determine whether there indeed was a conspiracy. In the latter stages of the investigation John Deane was ordered to interview an Englishman who had sailed on one of the three vessels bound for Cadiz. The interview took place in London in November 1727. The name of the Englishman was Mr Young. It had been Mr Young that Deane had spoken to in Elsinore when he had first observed the Russian ships two years previously.

Deane asked Young what was on the ships.

Young replied: 'Anchors, cables, cannon, small arms, shot, shells, tallow and tarr'. Despite the presence of weapons and ammunition this was not an arms stash, but rather a 'naval store'.

Deane wanted to know what Young's commanding officers had thought about him and what he was doing in the vicinity.

Young replied that they thought Deane's business was, 'to settle a correspondence as a merchant'.

The Russians' route to Spain was indirect and therefore suspicious. Deane wanted to know why they went 'north about'.

Young explained that it was the commander's orders 'to go north about' in order 'to avoid the channel'.

The ships had put in on the Irish coast. Was this by 'design or necessity'?

Necessity, Young said. There had been 'very bad weather'. Young's ship had lost its fore-topmast and had been forced to refit.

In that case how did the Russian officers 'behave to those of His Majesties Customs when they came onboard?'

Compliant, Young replied.

Did the Russians 'correspond with, or receive visits from any people of fashion on that coast?'

'Gentlemen of fashion did come aboard,' Young said but he 'was never admitted to their company'.

'Were there any arms or ammunitions delivered from your ship while on their coast, or did you observe any such design, had they met with proper persons or opportunities?'

Young said no, 'nor could I observe they put in shore with any other design than to refit.'

'When you arrived at Cadiz, did officers immediately go about delivering their goods and receiving others in order to get home before their ports should be frozen up?'

Young stated that the Russians took their time. They received a cargo of salt to take back to Russia. 'There was no haste made to leave this port because they designed to winter in Ireland.'

Deane wanted to know if any British or Spanish 'persons of rank' had visited the Russian ships.

Young answered yes on both counts although he didn't know who they were.

The interview continued.

Deane turned his attention to Young and company's journey home and the fact that the three ships had put into the Spanish port of St Andero.

'Where did your commander purpose to winter, or was it a design or necessity to put into St Andero?'

The commander's plans had been to winter in Ireland if the weather was bad. As it had stood the weather was fine, enabling them to sail on to St Andero without interruption.

'Had you delivered all your goods at Cadiz or did you deliver and receive any at St Andero?'

'We unloaded our ships at Cadiz and took in nothing more than provisions.'

'Did you not touch on the Irish or Scottish coast on your return?'

'We saw no land from St Andero.'

Mr Young's inconclusive testimony joined the glut of intelligence that trickled back to Walpole and Townsend from a series of creditable sources in Europe. The consensus was that no invasion was imminent. Townsend was not convinced by the increasingly overwhelming evidence to the contrary and carried on in his paranoia trying to connect dots that did not exist.

John Deane's interview with Mr Young was his last contribution to the invisible war that had quietly raged between Great Britain and Russia. With the interview completed, the state of Russia was now no longer his concern. He had a new post and new responsibilities. John Deane was bound for Ostend.

Part Four

Statesman

18

Water for Wine

*E*ighteenth-century Flanders was a country with something of a divided personality. At the beginning of the century Flanders had languished under Spanish control. In 1713, at the conclusion of the War of Spanish Succession, control of Flanders had passed from Spain to Austria.

Now that a sort of peace had descended on the country, as far as Austria was concerned, Flanders' numerous ports could be properly utilised for trade. The target was East India. Since the sixteenth-century, England and Holland had exerted dominance on trade in East India. Now Austria was keen to establish an East India Company in the Flanders port of Ostend. Austria established trade deals with the French and the Spanish, and the Ostend East India Company was formed. England and Holland made their disapproval known. They virtually threatened Austria to desist and forced the new company to dismantle itself. Consequently the Ostend East India Company was given a period of seven years to put its house in order and then disappear. So that it did not lose money, the British and the Dutch extended one concession to the company. The company was permitted to conduct a maximum of two trading voyages to India for every year of the company's remaining existence.

Naturally the British government did not trust Austria to uphold their end of the enforced agreement, so John Deane's covert agenda as the commercial consul for the ports of Flanders and Ostend was to report to Lord Townsend anything that might threaten British interests in East India. And although Townsend's concerns about a Russian-backed Jacobite invasion of Britain had proved something of a fever dream, the Jacobite threat was still a cause for genuine concern.

There was a powerful Irish presence in Ostend, many of whom were suspected Jacobites. John Deane was the obvious person to report on and frustrate Jacobite designs.

Deane's official duties were essentially to police trade and collect revenue from the British mercantile community. Part of the revenue took the form of 'consulage', a tax every British ship had to pay in port; a tax from which John Deane would take his wages. Deane's other main consideration was to make certain that the merchants' paperwork was in order. The obstacles facing John Deane were the mercantile community's resentment of what they perceived to be needless and restrictive bureaucracy and their reluctance to pay consulage. Traditionally, getting merchants to pay consulage was like pulling teeth. Deane's situation would be not helped by the fact that previous consuls had been principally decorative, wealthy by other means and conflict averse. Consequently they had hardly bothered to collect what was their own and their government's due. There was another reason for merchants not wanting a consul to look too closely into their affairs. Smuggling was an endemic problem in the ports of Flanders.

In addition to the regulation of his own countrymen, a consul's duties involved dealing with the aggressive trade policies of the host nation. In March 1728 the Flemish authorities in Nieuport had charged the master of an English vessel a brokerage fee of three gilders despite having 'transacted no business with him'. When he contested the matter he was arrested. In contrast, Dutch ships were completely exempt from such vigorous brokerage despite often having more cargo. Around about the same time an English merchant ship transporting a cargo of grindstones, coal and bottles had sold its entire load to a single Nieuport merchant. The Nieuport merchant made a contract with the English merchant for three more voyages transporting the same cargo. The Nieuport magistrates blocked the voyages and insisted that from that point on all ships had to sell their goods by auction. This was the world that John Deane had inherited.

None of this would have overly concerned Walpole and Townsend in their appointment of John Deane. In Deane they had a tenacious,

flint-headed man with a wildly puritanical streak. They were confident that not only would Deane continue his outstanding run as an
intelligence officer, he would reform an endemically corrupt port,
long overdue a reckoning.

Deane would indeed execute his duties with single-mindedness.
But in John Deane, single-mindedness was a quality that was char-
acteristically double-edged. He would fulfil his orders, official and
covert, scrupulously. But with his genius for conflict Deane would
soon count numerous Flemish nationals among the increasingly
lengthy roll call of people who hated him. He would antagonise his
own countrymen. He would frustrate his peers and his superiors. In
time, John Deane would even earn the rebuke of the king of England.

John Deane arrived in Ostend in April 1728. He began to get the lie
of the land and it did not take him long to determine whom his future
enemies were likely to be. Among the fractious community Deane singled out a Mr Lee, a prominent merchant whom Deane described to
Townsend as an 'Irish papist deeply tainted with Spanish zeal'.

John Deane's first task was to introduce and sustain a system of
regular consulage payment. Deane had inherited a mess. The British
merchants who used Ostend had been in conflict with the previous consul over the matter of consulage. Now that John Deane
was among them, the merchants held a general meeting to discuss
how consulage was to be regulated for the future. Whatever the
merchants' proposals were, John Deane was not happy with them
and was disinclined to consent to their wishes. Deane discussed the
matter publically and privately with Mr Lee. Deane made it clear
to Lee that it would be his fault if the two men could not 'live well
together'. There was additional tension with Lee over a pass for a
ship that Deane was reluctant to grant. Deane suspected that Lee was
trying to circumvent his authority and get a pass granted from the
admiralty office by alternate means.

Deane needed allies to do his job properly. He had Townsend's
support in London. He had the advocacy of Robert Daniels, the
English minister in Brussels whom Deane praised to Townsend for
his assistance. But Deane needed the aid of the governor of Ostend,

the Marquis De Campo. De Campo's support hung in the balance. In Deane's opinion, Mr Lee had an undue amount of influence over De Campo. But Deane was convinced that he could secure De Campo's loyalty. The two men met. They had a long conversation. They got on well. De Campo told Deane that he required documentation specifying 'what consulage each ship ought to pay, and that Mr Lee would see the same executed'. De Campo agreed to speak to the merchants on Deane's behalf.

Further tensions between Deane and Lee developed over a ship in port named the Mary Galley. The ship was bound for Cadiz. James Fitzgerald, the master of the ship, had gone to London. Another man arrived in Ostend to command the Mary Galley. The new master was Lee's brother-in-law. He wanted his pass endorsed by John Deane. There were problems with the pass. The pass had been altered. Another ship's name had been erased and the name of the Mary Galley had been written on the erased section of the document. Although Deane did not believe the documents were genuinely fraudulent he was still reluctant to endorse the pass to the ship's new master. Lee contested the decision. From Deane's point of view it was imperative that he had his way in this matter. Deane wrote: 'If Lee gains his point in this, I have little reason to expect doing any good here … '. Deane was further exasperated to learn that Fitzgerald had been told by Lee that he shouldn't pay the standard consulage from Spain. Fitzgerald was not the only one who believed he was exempt. When John Deane made his first attempts to collect his due he met with flagrant opposition. A Mr Howells refused point blank to pay. Deane had him arrested. John Deane had been in Ostend for less than two months and he was already embroiled in a power struggle he could not afford to lose.

Almost as soon as Deane had arrived in Ostend he had applied to Townsend for permission to return home. He cited 'an unsettled condition which my family is divided'. Deane returned to Nottingham in May to resolve his elliptical family problems. In England he met with the attorney general and discussed the problem of consulage. As the situation stood, John Deane could only force defiant merchants to pay consulage by taking them to court. But Deane was not confident the local courts would necessarily back him. He needed letters from Townsend officially empowering him to collect consulage. He wanted the letters to be delivered to the merchants of Ostend and Bruges en masse at a general meeting. He wanted the letters to contain a sentence of rebuke to the merchants for, 'flying in the face of government and very ill becoming good subjects'. Deane was due to return to Ostend in September. He fully intended to come back armed with everything he needed to bend the merchants to his own and His Majesty's wishes.

John Deane described his return journey to Ostend as, 'disagreeable, tedious and expensive'. He was overcharged at customs despite having with him, 'nothing new and only necessaries'. In Deane's absence a merchant had died. Deane was provided with the dead man's house as his new home. Deane paid the Marquis De Campo a visit. He was warmly received. De Campo asked after Townsend, 'of whose health,' Deane observed, 'he never omits enquiring'. While the two men were talking, a third entered. He was the new burgermaster. His name was Mr Ray. Deane had not met him before but knew of him; he did not approve of him and would accuse him to Townsend of, 'strenuously opposing everything that tends to the honour or interests of His Majesty or Protestant Britain'.

Mr Ray and Mr Lee were friends and compatriots. Prior to Deane's departure for England, Ray had bought a ship for Lee and had begun fitting it out for a voyage to Cadiz. The ship was in a bad condition and the work was shoddy. The practice of fitting ships 'to be no more than is necessary to preserve them from perishing' was endemic in Ostend and met with John Deane's disapproval. Now that he was back in Ostend, Ray applied to Deane for help in acquiring a pass for such a ship. Deane was not impressed and determined to subject the ship to a thorough inspection.

Despite initial hostility, John Deane was optimistic about the prospect of change for the better. In addition to Townsend, Robert Daniels and the Marquis De Campo, Deane had received a pledge of support from his old friend Sir Charles Wagner. The English admiral promised to do 'everything in his power to facilitate the impending affairs here'. A meeting of the merchants of Bruges and Ostend had been arranged to address the problem of consulage. Deane believed Bruges was something of a lost cause but was confident he could make the merchants at Ostend see sense.

All the while, Deane continued to work as an intelligence agent. He acquired access to some of Ray's correspondence from a company manager at Antwerp. He unearthed intimations that a count had 'discovered the resolutions of England and Holland to sink or burn all ships of this place that they should meet beyond the cape … '. Deane also learned that a French cardinal believed that 'Europe could expect no peace' while the Vienna alliance survived. John Deane passed the information on to his superiors. Deane assumed that attempts would be made to read his own mail and took measures to assure that this did not happen.

Deane's meeting with the merchants took place in Bruges. There was debate. There were the inevitable tensions. As expected, Mr Lee opposed John Deane. The discussion was heated. Deane felt his temper rise but was able to suppress it. He now possessed the letters from Townsend that he needed to validate his demands for consulage and this seemed to begrudgingly settle the matter. Deane assured his superiors that he was now determined to 'retrieve the government's honours and interests'.

Outwardly John Deane could project immense confidence, bull-headedness and strength as he prosecuted his duties. But the old private fears of destitution and financial ruin gnawed away at him. Deane was worried that his fortunes were so inexorably linked to the favour of Lord Townsend that, should the secretary of state die, he would not be supported. Ironically, now that he was properly authorised to collect it, consulage became a real source of anxiety. Consulage was Deane's only source of income, yet the amassed earnings he was entitled to were meagre in comparison to the financial demands of his rank and position. In Ostend, a man's status and authority was linked to his ability to reciprocate hospitality. If Deane were invited to a person of influence's house for dinner he was expected to respond in kind or risk a belittling of status. In Ostend, status and authority were conjoined twins. Deane put it this way: 'If I ate a bit of meat or drink a glass of wine at another's house, I must return it, and not water for wine.' Whether he made up the shortfall in his earnings by borrowing or dipping into personal savings is not known, but by the closing months of 1728 John Deane complained of being £200 'out of pocket on this account'. From now on, the formal and deferential tone of much of Deane's subsequent correspondence with his superiors would often be upended by a tormented sentence or paragraph bewailing his purgatorial financial state.

As Deane continued to do his job as both consul and spy, the winter unfolded in a series of conclusive incidents and dramatic non sequiturs.

Deane worked with De Campo to introduce the practice of ships displaying their country's colours when coming in and out of port.

Deane arrested the Irish master of an English-built ship but let him go.

Deane passed on information to the admiralty about a man named Robert Smith who had snuck in and out of port without paying the British government what he owed it.

Deane passed on information received from the director of post that it was known that commissions were being given by the British 'to destroy' Ostend Company ships, 'if found attempting to go to India'.

Deane passed on his suspicions about a ship called The Seahorse that was 'cargoed with a host of mysterious secrecy'. Onboard was a Captain Combs who had a price on his head for shooting a customs officer in England.

There was some consternation about a sixteen-gun frigate that had been spotted at Dunkirk. Deane met three men outside the walls of Ostend who provided him with information about the frigate.

Mr Ray complained about a pass that he had hoped Deane would grant him that Deane admitted to his superiors Mr Ray had 'little hope of seeing'.

The relations between Deane's allies became strained, manifest in a rift between Robert Daniels and the Marquis De Campo. Tension was endemic. 'Jealousy and suspicion abound here,' Deane reported. He complained that, 'I am frequently cursed by drunken sailors', and that, 'some of better fashion whisper as I pass by'. Deane was convinced that there were elements in Ostend that were trying to glean information about him through his servant. His public response to all of this was to look unconcerned and avoid 'all disputes or giving offence'. Privately, Deane wilted. He seemed particularly upset that his vast naval experience had failed to win him any respect or confederacy among fellow seafarers.

In December rumours spread around Ostend that the English king was dead. John Deane had to write home to confirm that this was not the case in order that he might scotch the incendiary gossip. A ship that Deane was convinced was a smuggling vessel left Ostend. The boat was supposed to be transporting tallow but it took two men to row a single cask aboard, effort not commensurate with the cargo. The cargo was loaded between midday and one o'clock in the afternoon, the time when virtually everybody in Ostend was sitting down to dinner. Deane believed that the illicit cargo was money. He passed the information on to his superiors.

Deane's own relations with the Marquis De Campo showed signs of wear and tear. Deane complained of De Campo's neglect regarding certain matters of harbour management. Deane had tried to instruct De Campo as to the correct manner in which he should be going about his duties. He had received De Campo's assurance that he would put Deane's instructions into practice. Nothing was done. Deane felt frustrated.

A degree of mutual suspicion had infected the relationship between John Deane and the Marquis De Campo. It needed to be dealt with. De Campo liked English food. Deane arranged a dinner for De Campo. By necessity, also present at the dinner was the despised burgermaster and his wife. The dinner was a partial success, easing the tensions between Deane and De Campo but at the expense of a portion of John Deane's pride. Deane was forced to humble himself, bite his tongue and weather a degree of gentle derision from his dinner companions. Deane's religion was the subject up for ridicule. Deane complained that he was 'teased' regarding the state of his soul. He tried to change the subject. He swallowed their mockery for diplomacy's sake but took solace in the private contempt he felt for their primitive grasp of theology.

As 1728 ended and the New Year commenced, Deane's financial position had not changed. He complained once again to his superiors about fiscal circumstances he described as 'miserable'. He asked for money or credit. Deane's concerns had become increasingly dominated by finance and his correspondence with Lord Townsend took on an unprecedented, increasingly bold and indignant tone. He invoked his years of service to Townsend in a virtual demand for redress: 'and that I, after being seven years under your Lordship's patronage, and desiring only bread, should be neglected is really very grievous, being confident that on every occasion I have, even at the hazard of my own life, obeyed your Lordship's commands'. Deane concluded his letter to Townsend with an apology for the nature of his request for money. But the flavour of the apology was tokenistic, Deane's sense of betrayal temporarily outweighing any sense of deference to his patron.

The beginning of 1729 was a period of stasis brought on by hostile weather conditions. The winter weather was fierce. Trade had virtually ground to a halt. Hardly any English ships had bought or sold anything. The only news that John Deane felt fit to report concerned a tobacco ship that had come to grief when it had run aground.

In February the winter was still holding commerce to ransom but by March John Deane was embroiled in a fresh controversy. A Dutch court had banned imports of grain. On a personal level the news did not particularly concern Deane as grain was not an enormous English export. But Deane was obliged to play his part martialling a legal response to Holland's aggressiveness. The actions of the Dutch courts unified a normally fractious community. English merchants and Dutch merchants affected adversely by the court order were bonded in opposition to it. John Deane was all of a sudden useful to the community he had been at perpetual loggerheads with. He tried as best he could to collate everyone's grievances in a single petition, confident that the courts would overturn the Dutch embargo.

By March, tensions had not abated. Three English ships had been seized. The ships were released but their cargo of corn was retained by the Dutch. On top of this, John Deane had to field the new influx of tittle-tattle doing the rounds in Ostend. According to the rumour mill this time, British-ruled Jamaica had fallen to the Spanish.

As John Deane reached the end of his first year in Ostend his principle concern was neither the state of Jamaica or English grain exports. It was, as it had been from the beginning of his tenure, money. Deane had performed his duties faithfully, and for the most part successfully. But he was virtually penniless. Deane had been forced to let a valued servant go who had been in his employ for a decade. The loss of the servant further reduced his social status, engendering diminished respect among his enemies and his peers. He wrote yet another impassioned plea to Townsend asking for money. The tone was less accusatory than his last correspondence on the subject had been. It was heartfelt but there was a thinly veiled ultimatum, albeit one born of genuine desperation:

> So if your Lordship don't please in some way to consider and assist me, I must of necessity soon follow, for I freely own I cannot be content to spend the rest of my days here in indolence which appears to me like dying by inches, and leave either myself or my family exposed to beggary in old age.

19

The Duke of Lorraine

J ohn Deane served in Ostend for ten years. Less than halfway through his tenure things had changed for the better and for the worse. By 1731 Deane had won his battle for wages. On top of the consulage he was allowed to collect, Deane was paid £200 per year plus expenses. Deane had brought a considerable degree of reform to Ostend. The consequence of reform was unpopularity and enemies. When harried and besieged, John Deane could always rely on the support of Lord Townsend; even when they disagreed. Even when John Deane overstepped the mark in terms of propriety, the bond was always a strong one and difficult to sunder. But Townsend had fallen.

Walpole and Townsend's relationship had been gradually disintegrating. Townsend's wife had died. The end of the blood bond that united the two statesmen placed something of a distance between them. The second catalyst for the rift was Townsend's deep-seated belief in an alliance with France as the key to Britain's stability. The alliance had been established by the Treaty of Hanover at the conclusion of the War of Spanish Succession. From Walpole's point of view the treaty was a temporary pragmatic necessity, not something to be clung to in perpetuity. Townsend believed in the treaty as if it were holy writ. From Walpole's perspective Townsend's attitude lacked forward thinking and was somewhat fossilised. For Walpole, political flexibility was the key to the nation's survival and prosperity. If Townsend were to remain entrenched with regard to the Treaty of Hanover then he was of no more use to Walpole.

The prime minister would not move directly against Townsend but he would not support him as he had done in the past. Townsend's constant banging of the drum for the Treaty of Hanover was gradually alienating the majority of his political contemporaries. All Walpole had to do was withdraw his patronage and protection, and wait for Townsend to step down when it became obvious to the secretary of state just how isolated he had become. Townsend's political career ended when he lost the confidence of the king. The catalyst was a public argument between Townsend and the duke of Newcastle. When the king sided with Newcastle, Townsend resigned and retired to Norfolk. Townsend was replaced as secretary of state for the north by William Stanhope, the 1st Earl of Harrington.

Lord Harrington had inherited John Deane, he hadn't recruited him. From Harrington's perspective the relationship between the two men would be more formal, distant and professional. Harrington would be subject to the sort of demands for redress that Deane had routinely laid at the feet of Townsend. Deane's future complaints would be listened to and weighed fairly but Deane would not be indulged in the same way he had been by Townsend. And John Deane would learn to his cost that there was a point beyond which even he could not push.

Deane's last great fall from grace took place in the autumn of 1738. He would be permitted one final triumph before his life of adventure ended for good.

By the summer of 1731 John Deane had settled into the role of a spectacularly unpopular man representing the interests of a resented nation. Deane had just returned from France and had almost immediately run into conflict with the packet boat, the ship that transported and delivered mail between Ostend and England. Deane had sent a man to the packet boat with a letter for a Mr Casey, the mate onboard. Casey was instructed by Deane, 'for the good of His Majesty's service not to proceed to sea with the mail you may expect this day, but wait till you hear further from me'. Deane punctuated his order with a threat: 'Your compliance here is expected as you will answer the contrary at your peril.' The letter went on to order Casey not to talk to his compatriots about why he had delayed the packet boat. Deane's reason for ordering the packet boat to be delayed was that he was waiting for intelligence from another boat and, if the intelligence necessitated a response, he wanted to send a letter to Lord Harrington as quickly as possible. Casey's response was to ignore Deane's orders and set sail at the proper time. Deane summoned Casey to give account for his disobedience. Casey ignored Deane's summons.

Both Deane and Casey represented the interests of Great Britain but each man clearly hated the other. The rest of Ostend seemed united in their mutual fear and suspicion of the English. Feelings towards the English were hostile at the best of times but the presence of an 'English frigate and Brigantee' at Dunkirk inflamed existing hostility. Despite the presence of the English navy at Dunkirk, Deane reported that the British in Ostend were, 'much resented by all degrees of men here, as if the affront (as they call it) had been done to this place'. Deane perceived that ill feeling toward the British was such that Ostend would 'gladly come under' French rule. But concerns about internal divisions and international tensions were of secondary importance during summer 1731. One event eclipsed everything else. Francis Stephen, the Duke of Lorraine, and his wife were coming to Ostend. The Flemish port was in a mad state of preparation for the visit.

The Duke of Lorraine was visiting a number of ports in the Netherlands. The nature of the visit, at the duke's insistence, was incognito. There were to be no 'public honours' but nobody took the Duke of Lorraine's order seriously. Each port was keen to impress the duke and hopefully win his support and patronage. Each port sought to outdo the other in 'magnificent entertainments'.

While Ostend prepared for the advent of the Duke of Lorraine, John Deane was obliged to justify his actions in trying to delay the packet boat. Deane's decision had not been met with the universal approval of his superiors. Deane invoked his three decades' experience of giving and taking orders. In doing so he was asserting his right to make the kind of independent judgment he had just made if it was in the national interest. The fact that the packet boat's mate had defied him caused Deane to write a particularly strident assertion of his own moral superiority and right to be obeyed absolutely: '[…] and as to the mates, I have in my time commanded hundreds, not to say thousands such as they are, and shall for this day never put myself on a par with them'. Deane wrote on, invoking his faithful and often poorly rewarded service to two successive monarchs. He invoked his relationship with Townsend and the freedom the former secretary of state had afforded Deane in allowing him to give orders with the expectation of having them obeyed. Deane accused the packet boat trade of fraud on account of sending out more packet boats than was necessary. Deane quoted an official who had granted him permission to stop packet boats if necessity demanded it. He even cited a precedent where a packet boat had been stopped before. Deane waited for Harrington's ruling as to whether he had acted within or beyond his authority.

The Duke of Lorraine arrived in Ostend in August 1731. The British staged a mock naval battle in the harbour to amuse the duke. The duke was suitably entertained. The British took their turn wining and dining the duke. John Deane was present at the dinner and for a single evening was relieved of his pariah status.

The Duke of Lorraine knew who John Deane was. He sought Deane out and spoke with him for an hour. The duke knew about Deane's service in Peter the Great's navy. He knew about Boon Island. He asked Deane numerous questions and when he had finished his gentle interrogation the duke asked Deane if he might have a one of his Boon Island pamphlets. John Deane had had his *Narrative of the Nottingham Galley* reprinted in 1730 and presented the duke with a copy the following morning.

The duke was clearly taken with John Deane. He dovetailed in and out of Deane's company for the remainder of his stay in Ostend. Deane for his part was like a pig in mud. When writing up his account of his encounter with the Duke of Lorraine he tried to maintain a veneer of professionalism. Deane spoke of his being 'determined to be in the way and make what observations that I could', but could not help luxuriating in the status bestowed upon him by the duke and the annoyance it caused his enemies. He wrote, 'You'll be pleased to observe that all in the India scheme are extremely jealous of me …'. Deane's foreign enemies demonstrated their envy by neglecting to invite Deane 'either onboard the ships or to the townhouse'. It hardly mattered. Deane was able to spend more time with the Duke of Lorraine when the duke was entertained at Governor De Campo's residence.

As the duke of Lorraine prepared to leave the port, presents were exchanged. The duke received silk from the Company at Ostend. The duke distributed gifts, singling out those who had fought in the mock battle for particularly generous treatment. John Deane was pleased. He believed that his encounter with the duke meant that 'some use would be made (or at least attempt to be made) of his Highness in favour of this company'.

The entire encounter was replete with irony. In those few days Deane had proved more of a diplomat than any other Englishman present. What had facilitated his briefly exalted status was his legacy of cannibalism, survival and fighting for profit for a foreign king.

20

Irish Confederates and English Smugglers

1738 was John Deane's final year of employment. Once again he had reprinted the Boon Island narrative. It would be the last time in his life that he would republish his most favoured account of his best-known adventure. But there were no more aristocrats who would take an interest in a despised consul's antiquated feats of survival. By the year's end, John Deane would be finished. He would set fire to his last bridge, arresting any chance of further advancement. He would condemn himself to a long retirement in England. Deane had survived everything Boon Island and the Russian winter could throw at him. He had survived the mercurial whims of a treacherous tsar. The Swedes could not kill him at sea and the Russians and their Jacobite allies in the East had singularly failed to crush him on land. In the end, what finally did for Captain John Deane was a running dispute with the postmaster in Ostend.

Deane had, 'for eight years and odd months [...] lived in a friendly manner' with the postmaster. For two of those years John Deane lived directly opposite the postmaster's house. During that time, the postmaster had observed that many people came and went from Deane's residence on what appeared to be secret and possibly remunerative business. The postmaster offered his services to Deane. Deane promised nothing but encouraged the postmaster that he 'may on some future occasion' be of service to him. The day never came. In time, John Deane befriended and occasionally confided in the postmaster's brother. The postmaster felt slighted and from that point on began to regard John Deane as more of an enemy than a friend.

The first disquieting clue as to the postmaster's newborn hostility was a change in the hours that he did business. The postmaster altered the times he made up the mail for England. He ensured that English mail was sorted at the same time as the Irish mail, a practice John Deane felt deeply uncomfortable with.

In a very short space of time, Deane's relationship with the postmaster would take on the hue of a virtual blood feud. Deane referred to the postmaster in a letter as, 'malicious' and 'babbling'. Deane was convinced that there was a serious risk of the postmaster interfering with his mail. Deane also believed that there was a conspiracy among the postal service to keep him in the dark as to when the packet boat was about to sail. As a consequence, John Deane sent his letters to Lord Harrington via Calais. When the packet boat arrived, rather than wait for his post to be delivered to him via the postmaster, John Deane would collect his mail directly from the boat. When writing about his strategy for dealing with the postal service, John Deane circumvented the English minister to Brussels, Robert Daniels, in his dispatches, leaving him out of the loop and communicating exclusively with Harrington on the subject.

Deane continued to act as a spy. January 1737 saw 'more than an ordinary' amount of 'English ecclesiastics at this town'. Leading them was John Gould, 'an Irish papist.' Deane acquired a handwriting sample from Gould and the names of contacts in London Deane thought Gould was secretly corresponding with.

John Deane believed that the postmaster had delayed his mail on purpose. In early February Deane had sent a letter to a London agent containing a bill for £8 14s. He was disturbed to discover that the letter and the bill 'came not to hand till 24 February'. Deane believed that the postmaster had delayed the mail on purpose. It was the latest snipe in the war of attrition the postmaster appeared to have declared on John Deane.

In March, Lord Harrington told Deane that the king had given him permission to investigate Gould and the ecclesiastics.

The postmaster complained about Deane. He took issue with Deane's 'power to dispatch extraordinary packets', and his practice of receiving his letters 'directly from the vessels on arrival' – a practice that the postmaster found 'new and unprecedented'. In turn, Deane elevated the postmaster to an exalted place alongside Christopher Langman and Thomas Saunders as one of the most hated enemies and chief persecutors of his entire existence. Deane's verdict on his neighbour was that he had, 'born more ill treatment from this man, within these five months past than ever I bore from any private man in my life'.

Harrington and the king backed the postmaster. John Deane was ordered to send his mail through the proper channels and stop the 'dispatching of extraordinary packet boats'. Harrington ordered Deane to let the 'post master at Ostend have timely notice of your intentions'. Deane felt betrayed. He agreed to Harrington's first point but virtually refused to obey the second. He insisted that, 'I must, for very good reason, desire to be excused putting any letters of importance into this post office'. He launched into a rant in ink that dripped with self pity and hovered on the edge of instability. 'This evil strikes at my reputation,' Deane wrote. Deane's enemies were not just his enemies but 'the enemies of our country and religion, raging and laying schemes for my destruction'. He ended the letter by offering to fall on his sword if he had proved to be an unfaithful servant. And should Harrington accept his resignation there was, in Deane, the sweet prospect of release from his present sufferings: 'And as I, by this malicious representation must be rendered odious to my sovereign in whose cause I have long been a great sufferer, and am still daily […] I shall be happy to be relieved from Irish confederates and English smugglers.'

Harrington ignored Deane's offer to resign. There was very little censure or anger in Harrington's reply. He gently reiterated his instructions to Deane to obey him in matters regarding the postal service.

In March, John Deane was advised to act in defence of the English postal service when a packet boat was boarded by soldiers serving the Austrian emperor. The incursion was carried out on the pretext of looking for arms. The port master went straight to the Governor of

Ostend and complained. The Marquis De Campo was no longer governor. Deane had little confidence in his replacement, dismissing him as a near imbecile. 'Nothing can be said to the present governor that one would not say to a child,' Deane wrote. The governor laughed at the port master. Deane was personally incensed at the search. It was a direct challenge to his own authority as only he was authorised to board British packet boats and search them. Harrington agreed and supported Deane in his complaint.

In April, the governor fell ill and looked as if he might die. John Deane was apprehensive. He feared that the space left by the idiot governor would be occupied by a shrewd and ruthless Irishman joined at the hip to the hated local magistrates.

There were further abuses of English vessels. John Deane was an eyewitness to an incident in which a customs house officer tried to seize an English captain's expensive hat. The captain slashed his hat with a knife rather than let the customs officer take it. Deane reported the incident to Harrington.

Deane would always act in favour of the English postal service when interfered with by a foreign power. But he still hated and mistrusted them and would seldom pass up an opportunity to belittle them to Harrington. Robert Daniels gave Deane a letter for safe keeping, prompting Deane to comment to Harrington on the irony of being entrusted with a letter when he was obstructed from 'corresponding with safety'. Deane made reference to seamen actually being searched for letters he might have passed on to them. Deane corresponded with Harrington via the wife of a shipmaster in Dover, completely circumventing the Ostend postal service in direct defiance of Harrington's wishes. Deane even admitted it to Harrington, his rationale being, 'were it not for this it would be impossible to send it'. If Harrington was displeased then so be it. 'Let the consequences be what it would,' Deane wrote.

The Irishman that John Deane feared would take the post of governor was Commandant Call O'Connor. The actual governor was still alive but by August, Call O'Connor was acting as the de facto governor in his stead. Deane disliked O'Connor for all the obvious reasons.

He was a Catholic. He was a Jacobite. He was a drunk. But Deane particularly disliked O'Connor for an unnecessarily brutal streak he possessed. A point of dispute between the two men exposed a softer side to John Deane than the one that was normally on display during his time in Ostend. Deane had interceded in the case of two young men who had been arrested and sentenced to death. Deane did not believe that what they had done merited the gallows. He talked to O'Connor and was left with the impression that he had convinced the commandant to spare their lives. O'Connor hanged them both.

Later that month, John Deane tried to send mail on the packet boat at the last minute, just before the packet boat sailed. The master of the boat refused to accept Deane's mail, even when shown written orders. Deane gave the mail to an associate named Mr Hall for a second attempt to get the letters aboard with instructions to proceed to Calais if refused. Mr Hall was allowed to conduct his business with the postal service.

In May, John Deane suffered further mail delays and excessive postage charges, the blame of which he laid at the feet of the postmaster.

In September, Britain was held up to public ridicule in the streets of Ostend. The king had fallen out with the prince of Wales and had banished the prince and his family from St James's Palace. The nature of the fallout was salacious ammunition to the enemies of the crown in Ostend. A manuscript arrived from England containing all the details of the humiliating rift in the royal family. Deane reported that the manuscript was read out 'publically upon the market places between the hours of eleven and twelve o'clock [...] to an audience of Irish and other enemies of our nation and government'. The crowd reacted with 'the greatest satisfaction'. The man who took it upon himself to read the document aloud was the postmaster of Ostend.

In April 1738 the liberties taken with British packet boats by foreign soldiers reached crisis point in an episode that threatened to become an international incident.

According to the British, one afternoon in Ostend, between three and four o'clock, the English packet boat was boarded by a stranger. The crew of the packet boat did not know the man. He was Irish.

The crew took him to be a sailor. The packet boat was approached by French soldiers. The soldiers boarded the vessel brandishing 'muskets, bayonets and swords', and took hold of the stranger. At some point John Deane was sent for. An officer of the packet boat ordered His Majesty's colours to be hoisted. As the stranger was being dragged away, an attempt was made to interfere with the arrest by John Howell, a member of the crew. He was thrust away with the butts of the French soldiers' muskets. In the middle of the confusion Deane had arrived and confronted De Graff, the soldier in command, on the waterfront.

'You are overstretching your powers greatly,' Deane said.

De Graff said nothing in response. Instead, according to Deane, De Graff made 'a flourish of his sword'.

The exchange played itself out in front of an audience of 1,000 spectators attracted by the chaotic spectacle. Howell and the man pursued onto the boat were locked up in the local gaol. The fugitive was cleared and released by the magistrates. Howell remained incarcerated.

The raid was interpreted as, 'violence offered to the king's colours'. It was a public slight to Britain. Lord Harrington wrote to Deane and Daniels. He assured Deane that he would do his best to seek proper redress. But the situation was complicated. Britain's moral high ground was subverted by the fact that it had technically sheltered Irish fugitives. There were potential criticisms levelled at John Deane from Harrington, principally that he should have ordered the crew of the packet boat to give up the fugitive. Deane defended himself by pointing to his normally appalling relationship with the postal service: 'They esteem me their enemy till in distress and they find no other friend.' Deane complained of the unclear nature of what his responsibilities were supposed to be. Was it his priority to protect British subjects or hand over deserters to the authorities? There was a lack of clarity in his official orders. There were contradictory orders circulating around the ports as to what British officials were to do with deserters, particularly deserters who had once been British subjects. There were written orders in Dover that stated that it was illegal for British dignitaries to give sanctuary to 'persons obnoxious to the government,' especially 'Irish deserters'. There were other slightly contradictory orders defining those denied sanctuary as 'deserters and other obnoxious persons'. There was vagueness to the definition that bothered Deane and made it difficult to know how to properly execute his duties. The normally draconian Deane displayed a liberal pragmatism when it came to certain deserters who had originally hailed from Great Britain. Deane felt that, rather than handing them back to the ruling authorities, they ought to be encouraged to return to Britain and enlist in its armed forces. The deserters were often well-drilled, capable soldiers who might otherwise be forced to fight for a foreign power and potential enemy of Britain. The most likely destination for fugitives would have been the Irish regiment in France. 'A good use may be made of these hard disciplined men at home,' Deane argued to Harrington. From Deane's perspective, to funnel so many soldiers back into a regiment so hostile to Protestant and Hanoverian interests was to sow into a whirlwind that Britain would surely one day reap.

Commandant O'Connor's version of the packet boat incident was predictably different from John Deane's. Banks, an Irish Lieutenant serving in the French army, entered Ostend on the hunt for deserters. He sought an audience with O'Connor. Lieutenant Banks questioned O'Connor about a certain deserter he believed was hiding in Ostend. When the two men had finished talking the lieutenant sent for De Graff. Banks requested that De Graff get five more soldiers so that they might accompany him to apprehend the deserter. The seven armed men marched to the English packet boat where Banks believed the deserter was hiding. De Graff asked John Howell to hand the man over. Howell refused. De Graff saw a boat approaching the packet vessel. He believed that the design of the boat was to ferry the deserter away. De Graff boarded the boat and arrested the deserter and then arrested Howell for obstructing him. Howell was imprisoned by the magistrates. The deserter was kept in gaol overnight and discharged the following morning.

O'Connor regarded Deane with a mixture of indifference and disdain. When he wrote up his own account of the packet boat incident he included a dismissive assessment of John Deane. He seemed to hold Deane in particular contempt for not talking to him face to face in the melee of recrimination and counter recrimination: 'This consul Deane has not vouchsafed to make the least complaint to me, as everybody does, but himself: I would not have failed doing everybody justice, whence I concluded his complaints frivolous.'

In June 1738 John Deane had met with a Captain Laye, who had been approved by Harrington as a deputy to Deane. His responsibilities were to act in Deane's stead when he was away from Ostend. Deane was not impressed with the captain and recommended the brother of the king's commissioner at Dunkirk, Daniel Day, as an alternative. Harrington approved the recommendation. Both Harrington and Deane were unaware of it, but between them they had selected Deane's future successor.

Lieutenant Banks was back in Ostend. Deane observed his movements. Banks met with two Ostend magistrates and Mr Ray the burgermaster at the townhouse. Together they searched through the records. A friend of Deane's asked Lieutenant Banks what he was looking for. Banks said that he was on official business to investigate the packet boat incident and find 'authentic certificates' that got to the bottom of what had actually happened because Banks feared 'England sought to make an affair of state of what had passed'.

Deane believed none of this. His own theory was that Banks was present 'in some Hibernian scheme for covering the commandant's conduct'. Deane also believed that O'Connor intended to sacrifice De Graff to censure and disgrace, in order to protect his own position. O'Connor and Banks were working closely together. Deane reported that on entering Ostend, 'all passengers that speak English, Scotch or Irish' were taken to O'Connor. Any suspect passengers among those brought to O'Connor were sent on to see Lieutenant Banks. John Deane requested that Banks be interviewed. The matter would not be resolved while Deane was still governor.

21

Abused by this Madman

On 4 September 1738 John Deane wrote: 'It is with great reluctance that I set about the following representation. But to be silent might I think be mostly esteemed a crime both with regard to His Majesty and the public service.'

Deane had sat down in hot blood to relay the details of a confrontation that had taken place earlier that morning.

At six o'clock the post from England had arrived in Ostend. The mail was transferred to the post office. Deane sent a man for his letters. The man returned empty-handed. The man had been told that the post office was closed. It wasn't certain when it would be open again.

At seven o'clock John Deane sent his servant to the postmaster's house wanting to know where his letters were. The postmaster replied that he would deliver John Deane's letters when he pleased.

Deane wanted his letters immediately so that he might quickly respond to any pending government business and send his replies back to England as soon as possible. The packet boat was due to leave Ostend between nine and ten o'clock in the morning. Deane wanted any replies that needed to be written to be on that boat.

Deane went to the see the postmaster in person. He asked why he was behaving in such a manner. The postmaster exploded at Deane. He demanded to know who had told Deane of the mail's arrival. The two men exchanged words. Deane sent 'a notary public' to 'protest' against the postmaster. The postmaster verbally abused Deane and then accused him of having perpetuated fraud by circumventing the Ostend postal service 'by sending a packet to be sent into the post office at Bruges for Vienna'.

The two men parted company.

Deane went home and wrote his letter to Harrington.

Concurrent to his dispute with John Deane, the postmaster had offended Ostend's magistrates. Almost immediately after his altercation with Deane, the postmaster had either been summoned before the magistrates, or else had encountered them. Either way he received a humiliating dressing down over, 'some unjustifiable practices on a letter of theirs'. The postmaster left the magistrates in state of near frenzy. He walked the streets of Ostend. His blood was up.

John Deane finished writing his letter at half past eleven. He would post it later. He left his house and went for a walk. He encountered a customs official. The two men talked. The postmaster was nearby. He saw Deane and the customs official and walked towards them. He saluted the customs official in French. He spoke to John Deane in English and cursed him. The postmaster walked away from Deane. He stopped. He walked back toward Deane, turned around and then walked away swearing. John Deane said nothing to the postmaster but put his fingers to his mouth. The postmaster placed his hand on his sword. The two men parted company.

Deane returned home and wrote a postscript to his letter describing the bizarre second encounter with the postmaster. Deane had had enough. He wanted Harrington to intervene conclusively in the matter of the unstable and obstructive postmaster. He wanted the postmaster's head on a platter. Deane sent the letter via Calais. Once again he made the decision to exclude Robert Daniels from the correspondence. Deane waited for Harrington's response.

After the exchange, Deane felt optimistic. The speed of the delivery of the mail had increased. John Deane credited his protest with the change in the mail service. Deane wrote to Harrington supplying him with further details of the postmaster's lunacies. He listed three reputable people, including his own wife, who had been 'abused by this madman'. Deane asked Harrington for an 'order' for the 'consul of Brussels, directing the magistrates of this town to examine under oath' witnesses present, mainly shop workers, who had observed the confrontation. Deane relayed to Harrington the gradual stages of his deteriorating relationship with the postmaster. He cited three people of good reputation who circumvented the postmaster to send mail, although Deane admitted that he was not certain whether any of them would 'stand to it when called'.

Harrington conducted his own investigation. He wrote to a certain dignitary for his opinion. The dignitary informed Harrington that the problem with the postmaster was that he did not come under British jurisdiction. The dignitary informed Harrington that the best person to sort the dispute out was His Majesty's minister at Brussels. But the dignitary was not convinced that taking the matter any further would serve any decent purpose. The dignitary offered Harrington his own assessment of Deane: 'I can have no opinion of the man,' he said, yet warned Harrington that John Deane 'may possibly give your Lordship trouble inconsiderably'.

Harrington brought the matter before the king. Harrington asked the king his opinion as to whether a formal complaint against the postmaster at Ostend should be made. The king was opposed. The king did not want his government to take action in something that appeared to him to be a personal matter. The king dismissed the complaint as 'to be of very little consequence'.

Deane received the disappointing news but felt inclined to push a little further. He got a letter from Whitehall. The letter stated that Harrington, 'was not disposed to trouble the king again'. It warned Deane that he would 'do well to drop the matter entirely'. It was a redundant warning. John Deane had overstepped the bounds of his authority one too many times. With the casual dismissal of a monarch, John Deane's career was over. He was recalled to England. He returned to his native country for the final time in October 1738.

John Deane was replaced as commercial consul for the ports of Flanders and Ostend by Daniel Day, the man he had personally recommended to Harrington as his deputy.

Deane's last letter to Harrington was brief, formal and humble in tone:

I promise, God willing, to embark with my family for England this evening and from the first convenient place of landing shall make the best of my way to Wilford near Nottingham where your Lordship's commands will always find me.

Part Five

Survivor

22

1746

The irony of John Deane's dismissal was that it had left him financially secure for perhaps the first time in his life. Deane's service was rewarded with a generous government pension. By the time of his retirement, John Deane was wealthy enough to buy land, build property and collect rent. Financial security was arguably all John Deane had ever really wanted. He had never sought to be famous. His adventures had always been a means to an end. Whenever John Deane had been dragged into the limelight it was usually by tragic default. It took him an age to learn the value of self-publicity and when John Deane had revealed in print the intimate details of his extraordinary life after Boon Island, it had been mostly in state documents never intended for public consumption. John Deane was an extraordinary writer but a reluctant one it seemed. In his government dispatches he never gave any personal details beyond those pertaining to the task in hand. No family correspondence of John Deane's appears to have survived. No contemporary likeness of him exists. The rest is semi-darkness, a prosaic pastoral existence interrupted by the odd moment of extreme drama.

Four elements had propelled Deane through a lifetime of adventure: the need to make money, a genuine sense of duty, an authentic (if somewhat Old Testament-inflected) Protestantism and a finely tuned instinct for conspiracy. The latter element dovetailed with a paranoid streak that had ultimately neutered John Deane's usefulness as a government employee. In his time, Deane had seen plots and conspiracies both where they had existed and where they had not. His enemies of choice had always been the Jacobites. His public and private nightmare was a Jacobite invasion of his beloved homeland.

He had successfully exposed Jacobites but had also been written off as a demented Cassandra. He had investigated indistinct and phantom Jacobite plots at the behest of a paymaster more obsessed than even he appeared to be. So there must have been a perverted sense of vindication when, in 1745, all of Deane's fears took substance in the form of a Jacobite army travelling unopposed through England and marching towards Nottingham.

In 1743 Charles Edward Stuart, the son of James III, arrived in Scotland with foreign backing. The French had provided two warships to take the Stuart prince to Scotland. The ships were badly mauled by storms, compromising what help the French had offered. But Charles Stuart was physically present on British soil and soon became a flesh and blood rallying point for the Jacobite Highland clans. Over the course of the following year, Charles Stuart began to build an army and won a victory over Hanoverian forces at the battle of Prestonpans.

In England, as an army was being assembled to take the fight to Scotland, Nottingham played its part in providing soldiers for the oncoming conflict. The Duke of Kingston had raised 200 mounted troops, many of whom were recruited from Nottingham. The soldiers were paid for by the town's aristocracy and its wealthy citizens. Kingston and the Duke of Newcastle gave £1,000 each. Lords Middleton, Byron, Howe and Cavendish gave £200 each. Other wealthy gentlemen from the locality donated £200. John Deane was among the contributors. The recruits were physically short men as a dragoon could not be taller than five feet eight. Many were butchers' apprentices. The recruits would become Kingston's 10th Light Horse.

On 12 October 1745 Nottingham's market place filled up with soldiers. The regiment constituted 500 Dutch soldiers and 200 English. On 13 October the regiment advanced towards Scotland.

In November 1745 Charles Stuart felt empowered and emboldened enough to march on London. He led 5,000 men across the Scottish border and into England. The soldiers making their way north and their enemies marching south seemed to miss one another. The Jacobites marched through Carlisle and Manchester on their

way to take London and oust George II from the throne of England.
By December, Charles Stuart and his Highland army had arrived at
Derby, less than fifteen miles from Nottingham.

Nottingham feared that it would be plundered. A wealthy
couple buried their valuables in an oat sack in their yard. Many in
Nottingham were angry that the local government had previously
dismantled its old siege defences.

Charles Stuart had hoped to ignite English Jacobite fervour
as he led his army towards the capital. He had hoped to arrive in
London with a great and well-armed host. But English Jacobites
stayed indoors, or else simply did not exist in numbers vast enough
to risk raising their heads above the parapet. Charles Stuart and his
Highlanders occupied Derby for two days before retreating from the
Midlands and marching back to Scotland.

On 17 April 1746 the two armies met at the field of Culloden.
By this stage in the conflict, Charles Stuart had withdrawn from his
own soldiers. He let them fight without him. What happened over
the course of the day simultaneously confirmed and negated the two
schools of thought regarding the Jacobite threat. On the one hand
the old Hanoverian nightmare had come true. The Jacobites were on
sovereign British soil with an army. On the other hand, the reality of
the Jacobite threat proved to be tragically overinflated. The Jacobites
were undisciplined, poorly equipped and divided among themselves.
It took the British Army one hour to slaughter their opponents, killing and wounding between 1,500 and 2,000 Jacobites, while losing
only 50 men. When the soldiers that John Deane had helped pay for
returned to Nottingham, they were lauded as heroes. A kettle drum,
a flag and a flagstaff would be placed opposite the entrance to the
council chambers to commemorate Nottingham's part in the victory.
Over 100 years later, in one of the Victorian chronicles of the history
of Nottingham, two butchers' apprentices were praised for having
killed 'fourteen of the enemy with their own swords' at Culloden.
The reality was far more squalid. Kingston's Light Horse were held in
reserve for a portion of the battle. When the clan McDonald broke and
ran, Kingston's Light Horse were sent in pursuit. They encountered

a group of Irish mercenaries who held their ground, kept their discipline and engaged the Light Horse. In electing to fight back, the Irish proved too fierce for Kingston's mounted soldiers. Kingston's men left the Irish alone and ran down and killed escaping Highlanders. Families of the Jacobite combatants were watching the battle. Kingston's mounted soldiers turned on them and killed women and children. They rode into Inverness and killed Jacobites there. Kingston's Light Horse carried on their murderous pilgrimage the length and breadth of the road to Inverness.

Whether John Deane knew what his money had actually paid for, or whether he embraced the official version of events is not known. His thoughts on Culloden are not recorded. But had he been fully aware of the atrocities he had funded, how would he have reacted? John Deane believed in honour in warfare. When Deane had fought in the Great Northern War he had held his ally, the Count de Buss, and the Italian mercenaries he had commanded in utter contempt for burning five timber boats and killing the crew. One can only speculate as to whether John Deane would have been able to arrest his deep-rooted hatred of the Jacobites enough to extend to their civilian dead the same military objectivity.

23

Mr Miller

There was one more moment of drama left for John Deane to endure. It was brief and created a final headline for the veteran of Boon Island. In 1748 John Deane was attacked and robbed on his own estate. The attack took place in daylight. The thief took everything of monetary value on Deane's person. Deane's coat sported some fancy sleeve buttons, which the thief cut off. The thief's Christian name was not recorded. His surname was Miller. He was arrested soon after the theft. He was tried, found guilty and sentenced to hang. Nottingham's executions invariably took place on a permanent scaffold just outside the town atop a ridge known as Gallows Hill. Miller was hanged publicly alongside a highway robber. Prior to death, it was customary to parade the condemned through the street in chains, either on foot or on the back of a cart. Hanging was a crude science in the 1700s. In Nottingham it meant being thrown off a cart with a short rope tied around the neck. Death would occur after approximately fifteen minutes of strangulation. A large crowd would always attend a public hanging. It is not known whether John Deane watched Mr Miller's execution.

A Mr Miller was hanged alongside a highway robber for a violent assault perpetrated on John Deane. *Illustration by Stephen Dennis*

Last Will and Testament

lthough Deane appeared to have written very little during this last period of his existence, there was one official document that cast small spots of light on his private life during his final years. In 1755 John Deane drafted his will.

There was a disjointed and fractious family to provide for. John Deane made provision for his sister Martha and her daughter Mary in the event that Martha died, the implication being that Martha was a widow as her husband was not mentioned at all. John and Sarah Deane had no children of their own. Deane made provision for his heir. Mary, John Deane's niece, the only surviving child of his brother Jasper, stood to inherit her uncle's estate when Sarah died. In the meantime, on John Deane's death, a yearly sum was to be paid to Mary from the interest on £100 from his estate. Deane seemed to regard Mary as profligate as the sum came with a warning to spend the money responsibly and not to 'waste it'. The conditions attached to Mary's children receiving money were strict. Mary's husband Edward, his children, and possibly Mary, clearly did not get on with Sarah Deane. There appeared to have been a serious dispute in the past. Consequently, once John Deane was dead, if Mary and Edward wanted their annuity, they needed to keep their distance from Sarah. A legal cordon was placed around Sarah to protect her. Edward and Mary were forbidden from venturing within 40 miles of John Deane's wife or they would not receive their money. Deane made arrangements to have the news of his death delivered to Mary and Edward, and the conditions of his will physically taken to them, a measure employed to prevent his relatives coming to Wilford and harassing Sarah Deane. Any money afforded to Mary and Edward's children was at Sarah Deane's discretion until the children reached their twenty-first birthdays.

John Deane made generous provision for Sarah. He referred to her in the document as, 'my beloved wife', and, 'my said loving wife'. Sarah was to receive 'all and singular my personal estate', and after tax, 'the rents of profits of all my said lands and tenements', so long as she remained a widow. But Sarah's remarriage or death would result in John Deane's trustees taking over the estate in the event that it had not been administered.

Deane set aside £5 to be distributed in the first month of every year among the poor of Wilford for as long as his wife was alive. Deane made it a condition of his will that whoever might buy his estate would 'stand up for the general interests of' the population of Wilford and 'not seek to oppress' them. His namesake and nephew John Deane Broughton, the son of his sister Martha, was to receive £20 to be paid within a year of John Deane's death.

Two years later, John Deane amended his will in the light of the death of one of his four trustees. He appointed a new trustee. But something seemed to have happened in the intervening time that obliged, forced, or provoked Deane to modify his previous generosity to certain family members. He reduced the amount of money he had ceded to his sister Martha. The £20 he had bequeathed to his nephew was altered to 'a few pounds and no more'. A sum of £100 from which he would give money to the poor was reduced to £25, although the poor of Wilford would still receive their £5 per year every January, presumably until the £25 ran out. Whether the changes in the will were necessitated by some alteration in his finances or whether he was punishing all and sundry for unrecorded offences is not currently known.

The events of Boon Island still weighed heavy on John Deane and he felt a powerful obligation to provide for one of the shipwreck's indirect casualties. Miles Whitworth was the son of Charles Whitworth, Deane's late friend and business partner. Miles Whitworth lived in New England. In his will John Deane arranged for £100-worth of goods to be bought in London and shipped to

America and given to Miles, presumably to sell or dispose of as Miles saw fit. Deane bequeathed three personal items to Miles: a silver hilted sword, three volumes of sermons and a pair of pistols. Deane placed great value on the pistols. He recorded in his will that the weapons had 'saved my life in the year one thousand seventeen hundred and twenty upon the River Volga'. It was a tantalising hint at a lost anecdote of close-quarter survival from Deane's time in exile transporting timber from Kazan to Lagoda Lake.

In August 1761 John and Sarah Deane died within a day of one another. There were no children to survive them. Husband and wife were buried together in St Wilfrid's cemetery. Their epitaph reads:

> Here lieth the body of John Deane, Esq, who from the year 1714 to 1720 commanded a ship of war in the Czar of Muscovy's service; after which, being appointed by his Britannic Majesty Consul for the ports of Flanders and Ostend, he resided there many years. By His Majesty's leave retired to this village in year 1738, where he died August the 18th, 1761, in the 82nd year of his age. His wife, Sarah Deane, lies here also interred who departed this life August 17th, 1761, Aged 81.

The tombstone makes no reference to Boon Island.

Epilogue

*I*n intermittent fits and starts, the potency of Captain John Deane's fame lasted into the twentieth century.

In 1762 Miles Whitworth reprinted the 1711 version of the Boon Island tragedy.

In 1870, the novelist W.H.G. Kingston wrote *John Deane: Historic Adventures by Land and Sea*. The novel was a work of fiction, an adventure story for boys. Anecdotes in the novel that had no basis in fact would soon be reported as true. For example, John Deane fought in the War of Spanish Succession under Admiral Sir George Rooke where he was promoted to the rank of captain. Deane was present at the liberation of Gibraltar. Deane feuded with his brother. The reason for the feud was revenue lost during the shipwreck at Boon Island. Kingston described the consequences of the disagreement as John and Jasper Deane walked across Nottingham to attend dinner at their sister's house:

> On their way, some remarks made by Dr Jasper irritated John Deane, as he considered them unfair and unjust, and angry words were heard by some of the passers-by, uttered by him to his brother. They reached the door together. A flight of stone steps led to it from the street. Unhappily, at this moment the doctor repeated the expressions which had justly offended the captain, who declared that he would not allow himself to be addressed in so injurious a manner. As he spoke he pushed impatiently past his brother, who at that moment stumbled down the steps. The doctor fell; and as Captain Deane stooped to lift him up, to his horror, he found that he was dead! Rumour, with her hundred tongues, forthwith spread the report that the fire-eating

captain had killed his brother. The verdict however of the jury who sat
to decide the case was, that Dr Jasper Deane had died by the visitation
of God.

Although it is almost certain that there was no truth in the story, the
anecdote became the most salacious tall tale believed wholesale by
those who would periodically excavate John Deane's history.

In 1899 John Deane's *History of The Russian Fleet during the Reign
of Peter the Great* was published by the Navy Records Society. The
society had no idea of the true identity of the document's author.

In 1917 the Jasper Deane account of the Boon Island shipwreck
was republished in *The Magazine of History and Biography.*

Kingston's novel went out of print. Deane's pamphlets were no
longer in circulation.

In 1934 John Deane was identified as the author of *History of the
Russian Fleet.*

In New England a renewed interest in John Deane was fanned
into flame by a local novelist. In 1956 Kenneth Roberts, a native of
Maine, wrote a fanciful but forensically accurate novel about the
wreck of the *Nottingham Galley* called *Boon Island.*

On Boon Island itself a few of the *Nottingham Galley's* cannons
were discovered by scuba divers. The cannons were resting on a ledge
25 feet below the surface of the ocean. In 1994 the University of
New England decided to remove the cannons, their decision has-
tened by a rumour that Massachusetts salvage hunters were on their
way to claim the antique weapons for themselves. The cannons are
the only surviving physical evidence that the *Nottingham Galley* ever
existed.

Kenneth Roberts' novel went out of print but was republished by
the University Press of New England in 1996. The new edition of
Boon Island contained reprints of John Deane's, Jasper Deane's and
Christopher Langman's accounts of their Boon Island experiences.
The novel fell out of print for a second time.

At the time of writing John Deane is probably better known in
New England than he is in his own country. In Britain he has been

largely forgotten when at one time, trailing only behind William Bligh's misadventure on the *Bounty*, the wreck of the *Nottingham Galley* was perhaps the most notorious English naval scandal of the eighteenth century. Even in Nottingham and its neighbouring Wilford village, John Deane is barely known. Two houses that Deane had had built in the 1730s still survive, yards away from the church in which he is buried. His tombstone is easy to find. The inscription is still legible but the grave rarely visited.

John Deane in Fiction 1

John Deane: Historic Adventures by Land and Sea by W.H.G. Kingston

In the preface to his novel W.H.G. Kingston cites an anonymous friend from Nottingham whose history of Deane's adventures provides the well from which he would draw material for his story. Kingston iterates that John Deane 'was a real person', implying that Deane's memory may have fallen out of fashion in the year of the book's publication. He provides a brief summation of Deane's life, background and principle exploits:

> He was born at that town A.D. 1679. Though of gentle parentage, in his early days he followed the occupation of a drover. He then went to sea, and became a Captain in the Navy; after that he was a Merchant Adventurer. He next took service under Peter the Great, and commanded a Russian ship-of-war. On leaving Russia, he obtained the post of British Consul at Ostend, held by him for many years. Returning home, he was made a Burgess of his native town, and took up his abode at the neighbouring village of Wilford, where, in 1760, he died.

All of the above is broadly true, although there is no mention of Boon Island. Having established a degree of historical credibility, Kingston immediately queers his own pitch by pointing readers to John Deane's tombstone and then entirely inventing a couple of inscriptions on it: 'His age, fourscore years and one,' and, 'After life's fitful fever, he sleeps well.' Kingston gets Deane's wife's name wrong, calling her Elizabeth. All of these errors could have been easily corrected by a quick look at the tombstone Kingston invokes. This mixture of fact and slip-shod inaccuracy establishes the tone for 415 pages of entertaining and outrageous nonsense.

The novel begins in 1696 with Rupert Harwood and his daughter Althea riding through Nottinghamshire on their way to visit the Deane family. Father and daughter are Jacobites. They discuss the Deane family, in particular the two brothers. Jasper is described as 'a quiet, proper-behaved young man'. John is described as 'a broad-shouldered lad […] not ill-fitted to fight his way through life'.

Father and daughter enter Nottingham where their passage is blocked by a mob baiting an ox. A lone man confronts the crowd. It is John Deane. The crowd nearly unhorse Althea. Rupert Harwood challenges the crowd, informing them that he is a justice of the peace. John Deane mitigates on the crowd's behalf, suggesting that formal legal proceedings are unnecessary but that he would be more than happy to track down the ringleaders and thrash them.

The Deanes live in the market place in the centre of Nottingham. The Harwoods and the Deanes dine and converse. They talk about John Deane's future prospects. John reveals:

> I should like to see the world, but I have not a fancy for knocking men on the head, and could never understand the amusement some people find in it; but I have no objection to stand up and defend my own if I am attacked, or to draw my sword in the defence of a friend or a right cause.

This is John Deane's philosophy of adventure that will be played out over the course of the rest of the novel.

We learn that Kingston's Deane is comparatively uneducated but not stupid. He likes weapons. He loves fishing. He is enamoured of the Robin Hood stories and believes them wholesale. He virtually hero worships his monarch William of Orange. He is an expert storyteller.

His favourite book is *Foxe's Book of Martyrs*. At the beginning of the novel Kingston's John Deane is a wild man tempered by a deep seam of decency and honour.

John Deane very quickly falls in love with Althea.

That evening Deane meets up with a gang of poachers that he runs with from time to time. Their plan is to steal fish. Deane's feelings for Althea trouble his conscience and he announces to his gang that this will be his last poaching raid. The raid is interrupted by the presence of Mr Pearson, a mysterious gentleman from Yorkshire. Pearson convinces the gang to let him accompany them. Pearson claims to be a cattle dealer but displays greater skill at poaching than Deane and his compatriots. When the gang are discovered and are fired upon by game keepers it is Pearson who guides them to safety. Pearson reveals that he knows who John Deane is. He is impressed with Deane and offers him work as a soldier for an unspecified cause. Deane politely declines and goes on his way determined to be more law abiding in the future.

Deane makes the decision to confess to his father his part in the poaching raid but a fire on a neighbouring property arrests his intentions. Deane risks his life and fights the fire. He becomes a local hero. The owner of the property offers to give Deane a start in business as a reward. It transpires that for a while John Deane has wanted to become a drover of cattle in order to see more of Britain. Deane is set up as drover's apprentice. As Deane is sent away on his first droving expedition he is advised by his cousin to trust in God, the first of many such endorsements by good, trustworthy Protestants throughout the novel.

Pearson and Rupert Harwood know one another. Both men are part of a plot to restore James II to the throne of England. It is Pearson and Harwood's intention to tempt John Deane over to their cause.

John Deane's adventures as a drover involve a trip to Stourbridge Fair, a dramatic run in with cattle thieves and an encounter with a Huguenot exile, expelled from France and separated from her husband and daughter. Deane experiences a string of encounters with Pearson, who criss-crosses his path. Deane is manipulated by Pearson into thinking that he is a wanted man for the poaching incident. Pearson convinces Deane that the safest place for him is either at Pearson's side or among Pearson's friends. Pearson sends Deane on numerous errands around the country. Deane hides out in the Fens and goes to London. He meets Elizabeth, Pearson's stepdaughter, an attractive Protestant who begins to challenge Althea Harwood for Deane's affections.

Without Deane fully realising it, Pearson gradually embroils and implicates him in a Jacobite plot to assassinate William of Orange. As the plot trundles on, Deane meets more prominent Jacobite conspirators and becomes more and more mired in the conspiracy. Just as the full horror of what Deane has become involved in dawns on him, the conspiracy is exposed and a retaliatory cull begins. Pearson slips away taking his wife and Elizabeth with him. Others are arrested and some are executed. John Deane manages to escape untainted but is burdened by guilt and feels the need to make amends. He enlists in the navy to prove his worth in military service and erase the shame of accidental treason.

It is about halfway through the novel. Up until this point W.H.G. Kingston has proved a fine storyteller. There are faults. The plot is stopped here and there for a history lesson better employed as a footnote. There are long-winded speeches. There are moments when normally shrewd villains are conveniently indiscreet whenever John Deane needs to overhear a crucial piece of information. But Kingston's faults are kept in check by his precision and vivid economy of description, his fast-moving and wry action sequences and an occasional gift for dialogue, whether it is a terse exchange in the middle of a fight: 'sheathe your blade, if you have not a fancy for having your brains blown out!', or John Deane's description of his own and his mount's mutual exhaustion after a long journey: 'I'm afraid if I were to ride on through the night with my tired steed, that we both of us should roll in the mud before day dawns.' Kingston's England is a wild, rambunctious, colourful and exciting place. Kingston's John Deane is complicated, changeable, honourable and corruptible. Even the villains are human. Pearson is likeable and displays a fondness for Deane even as he is attempting to pollute him. Deane feels a similar ambivalence about Pearson and despite his outrage can never fully bring himself to completely hate or denounce him. Pearson and Deane's relationship is reminiscent (perhaps to the point of plagiarism) of the reluctant friendship between the ideologically polarised fugitives Davey Balfour and Alan Breck Stuart in Robert Louis Stevenson's superior novel *Kidnapped*. Yet, once Deane joins the navy, the story begins to drown in its own sanctimonious ridiculousness.

The rot doesn't set in straight away. John Deane's first few naval engagements against the French are described brilliantly. There is grotesque detail, grim incident and black comedy. A man standing next to Deane is blown apart. Deane is covered in blood. He examines the dead man, unsure how much of the blood is his and how much belongs to the atomised shipmate. A sailor reassures him: 'See, that's his blood which has turned you into a red Indian.' It is a human moment laced with gallows humour. Deane is a cog in the machine. He is not yet a hero, merely an anonymous soldier playing his part in a glorious and awful event, observing the ways in which the seasoned and experienced deal with the appalling consequences of human behaviour. It is an incident worthy of the real John Deane. It is an anomaly in the writing of W.H.G. Kingston. From that point on the pace of the narrative accelerates. Deane goes from naval action to naval action. He rises through the ranks. He serves under some of the great admirals of the age. He wins their attention by being the first to volunteer for action. He boards a French galley and frees their slaves. He boards a privateer. He is given his first command. He dives into the ocean and rescues a drowning quartermaster who is about to be eaten by sharks. Deane's courage and modesty wins the devotion of his crew.

The novel begins to pile enough coincidence upon coincidence as to make even Charles Dickens embarrassed by the contrivance of it all. Deane liberates a slave who happens to be his beloved Elizabeth's father. The Huguenot he had met previously happens to be Elizabeth's mother. Deane and his crew are captured by pirates.

The pirate captain happens to be Pearson who happens to have Elizabeth stashed away on an island in the West Indies. Deane and Elizabeth are reunited and fall in love. The island is liberated by the British navy. Pearson gets away. The captain responsible for the rescue turns out to be Elizabeth's uncle. Elizabeth and Deane are parted once again.

Deane serves under Admiral Rooke. Once again he distinguishes himself in combat and earns further promotion. By this point in the novel, the battles begin to resemble history lessons as Kingston the pedant battles and triumphs over Kingston the storyteller. He seems to forget he is writing a novel about a man called John Deane and only tells the reader Deane's part in the battle as an afterthought rather than relaying the battle through Deane's eyes as he had done earlier in the story. And when Kingston allows John Deane centre stage in a military engagement, the result is ridiculous. The apex of Deane's military career is his part in Rooke's assault on Gibraltar. During the attack Deane volunteers to lead an attack on a fortress by climbing, 'a part of the cliff which the Spaniards had never thought it possible any human beings could climb'. But Deane manages it, taking prisoners and sparing Catholic women. Deane is promoted to captain. The flawed hero of the first half of the novel is now a martial saint, faultlessly courageous, perfectly honourable in combat and utterly boring.

All the while Deane longs for a respite in his adventures so that he can return to England and marry Elizabeth. When he finally gets the chance he discovers that Elizabeth is not in England. Elizabeth and her mother have been shipwrecked off the coast of New England. Deane wants to go to New England and find her. His need to see Elizabeth coincides with plans among his friends and relatives in Nottingham to trade in America. Deane agrees to captain a ship to New England. The ship is named the *Nottingham Galley*.

After thirty-four chapters W.H.G. Kingston finally tackles the incident that made John Deane famous. He devotes a little over a chapter to the Boon Island episode and seems to go out of his way to get every single detail wrong. The *Nottingham Galley* is manned by forty

sailors and protected by twenty guns. The voyage is 'prosperous' with
no intimation of any encounters with French privateers or discord
among the crew. The *Nottingham Galley* is bound for Delaware. When
it is just 50 leagues from the American coast a gale blows up. The
Nottingham Galley is driven onto the rocks of an island. Most of the
crew are drowned or die when they are 'dashed furiously against the
rocks'. John Deane is swept overboard. He is set on a beach. Apart
from Deane there are five other survivors. Deane and company
discover an abandoned shelter built from wreckage complete with
a door, a table, a shuttered window and silk, evidence of the presence of ladies. Deane discovers a Bible that belongs to Elizabeth. The
Nottingham Galley is lost but one of its boats has washed ashore. The
boat is intact but will let in water if the survivors try to use it. Casks
of food have been salvaged. Drinking water is a problem but not
for long. Deane discovers a tree on the island that yields moisture
seeping from its roots. Days pass and the food begins to run out.
A carpenter's chest is discovered between the rocks. It contains everything the castaways need to repair the boat. A ship is spotted. Deane
and company sail to meet it. It is a pirate ship manned by none other
than Pearson. After a tense exchange Pearson agrees to set Deane
ashore for old times' sake. Deane finds Elizabeth and is married. The
Boon Island episode is done and dusted without a single mention or
insinuation of cannibalism.

The novel is not quite finished. Kingston saves his most anomalous
detail for last. Deane returns home war rich from prize money but
having lost the investors their cash from the Boon Island adventure.
It is not Deane's fault but a contingent in Nottingham blames him
all the same. Jasper Deane is among them. Tensions between the two
brothers result in the argument that causes Jasper's death. John Deane
is legally exonerated but nevertheless held responsible by many in
Nottingham. The scandal is too much for Deane to bear. He accepts
an offer to travel to Russia with his wife in answer to a call for naval
talent by Peter the Great.

The death of Jasper Deane is such a throwaway piece of writing,
one wonders why Kingston included it. The anecdote does have

the faint ring of verisimilitude about it as it is so at odds with the pantomimic tone of the majority of what has preceded it. In reality, as his will attested, there were tensions between John Deane and his brother's daughter. Jasper's accidental death might have been the reason. More likely the story is a contrivance, devised as an alternate motive for John Deane to go to Russia so as to deflect attention from the historical reasons for his actual departure; accusations of fraud and stories of cannibalism.

The rest of Deane's career is given a jaunty spin by Kingston.

His time in Russia:

> He rendered great assistance in organising the navy of that wonderful man Peter the Great, and after serving with much credit for a few years, he returned to England.

His time in Ostend:

> Captain Deane had during this time found a number of friends, and by their means he was soon afterwards appointed English consul at Ostend, where he lived with his wife Elizabeth till they were both advanced in life.

Kingston portrays Deane's retirement in Wilford as a pastoral utopia:

> As an elderly couple they came back to Nottingham once more, and went to live in the sweet village of Wilford, on the opposite side of the silvery Trent. It was the peaceful green retreat that had beckoned him back to England from many a scene of foreign grandeur, and smiled across many a time of tumult and of battle.

W.H.G. Kingston was a religious propagandist. His novels were written to simultaneously entertain and instruct Victorian boys in morality and patriotism. They were published by Christian organisations. As liberally interpreted by Kingston, John Deane's life was the classic Prodigal Son story. So, having erred and repented, having been reborn as a knight errant, Kingston ends his novel with a blissful rendering of Deane's final internment complete with the promise of heavenly reward:

> The tomb of John Deane, Captain R.N., and of Elizabeth his wife, is to be seen on a little green promontory above the sparkling Trent and near the chancel of the parish church, where sweet strains of music, accompanying the sound of human voices and the murmurs of the river, are wont to mingle in harmonious hymns of prayer and praise. A more fitting spot in which to await in readiness for the last hour of life than Wilford can scarcely be imagined, nor a sweeter place than its church-yard in which the mortal may lie down to rest from toil till summoned by the last trump to rise and put on immortality.

Appendix 2

John Deane in Fiction 2

Boon Island by Kenneth Roberts

Kenneth Roberts' 1956 novel is an entirely more factually accurate account of the shipwreck than W.H.G. Kingston's panoramic fantasy. It draws scrupulously on the Jasper Deane, Christopher Langman and John Deane accounts for its details but is unashamedly partisan in favouring the Deanes' cause over Langman's. The majority of the story takes place during the ordeal on Boon Island. But Roberts allows himself a lengthy prologue in England, as bizarre in its own way as anything W.H.G. Kingston had written.

Boon Island's narrator is Miles Whitworth, an Oxford undergraduate with artistic aspirations. Whitworth hates being a student. He feels stifled by Oxford's moribund and ossified teaching practices. He would rather be a professional playwright. Whitworth's home is his beloved Greenwich by the River Thames.

Kenneth Roberts writes particularly well about London crowds, be it the bustle, business, colour and exoticism of the river traffic or the sounds and colours of a nocturnal theatre crowd. Roberts' descriptions of Deptford and Billingsgate are sensually rendered as he conveys the smells of the river and river industries.

Whitworth returns home. He tries to buy some whitebait from a young man by the waterfront. The boy's name is Neal Butler. He refuses to sell the whitebait to Whitworth because he has a pre-existing arrangement to trade his haul to a sailor named Christopher Langman. Butler and Whitworth talk. Whitworth learns that the majority of Butler's earnings come from the theatre. Butler works for a theatrical company for which he plays the female parts. Whitworth discovers that Butler's father is a semi-invalid sailor. After their conversation Whitworth observes Butler's transaction with Langman. Whitworth takes an instant dislike to Langman and immediately marks him as a troublemaker.

Miles Whitworth befriends Neal Butler. He meets Butler's father Moses who goes by the nickname 'Swede' on account of his striking blond facial hair. Swede is a crippled sailor currently employed as an actor manager. Swede wishes to see Miles Whitworth's father on a matter of business. Whitworth senior is a lawyer. At the Whitworth's home Neal and Swede Butler encounter Captain John Deane, who has gone to the Whitworths to insure cargo prior to a merchant voyage to America. As the men talk, Christopher Langman becomes the topic of conversation. Langman is John Deane's first mate. Deane dislikes Langman, whom he sees as a disreputable schemer. Unfortunately Deane is stuck with Langman. Langman owned a galley, which he claimed he had captured when he was a privateer. Langman had no money to pay his crew and was forced to sell the galley to cover their wages. He sold the captured vessel to John Deane on the condition that he be kept on as first mate. Deane is about to set sail. Langman has failed to retain all but two of his original crew. Deane sets about recruiting sailors for his upcoming voyage.

Over the next few days Miles Whitworth and John Deane spend time together. They attend plays. They watch Neal Butler perform on stage. They encounter Butler after an evening performance. He appears traumatised. Butler has been attacked by an amorous fop named Tintoretto. Although Roberts never openly states it, it is heavily implied that the motive for the assault is homosexual rape. Butler has killed Tintoretto in self defence but has left the body in a place where it can be discovered. John Deane removes the body and dumps it in a park. He takes Miles Whitworth with him. Miles is spotted by a theatre company member. Deane remains invisible. Deane fears that once the body is discovered it will not take long for people to connect the two young men to the death of Tintoretto.

If they stay in London Miles Whitworth and Neal Butler run the risk of arrest and trial. Charles Whitworth, despite being a lawyer, has no confidence that the English legal system is capable of giving the boys a fair hearing. Convinced of their innocence, Deane recruits them both as members of his crew in order to get them out of the country. Swede Butler signs on to look after his son.

As the *Nottingham Galley* sets sail Langman and his two lackeys Mellon and White complain about the state of the ship. They begin to spread rumours that John Deane has overinsured the cargo to the tune of £250. There are fears that Langman's design is to mutiny and seize back his old ship.

From this point on the narrative dutifully ticks off every significant moment from Jasper Deane, Christopher Langman and John Deane's original accounts of the shipwreck, always favouring Deane, always damning Langman. And if any indication were needed that John Deane had utterly defeated Christopher Langman in the propaganda war for his own reputation, the rest of Kenneth Roberts' novel is it. Roberts scrupulously favours Deane's version of events, acknowledging Langman's accusations but always framing them in the context of a conniving, plotting and unscrupulous mind. Langman spots what he believes to be privateers but is proved wrong. Langman organises a mutiny, which is only averted when John Deane beats him with a wig stand. Ultimately the sinking of the *Nottingham Galley* is Langman's fault. The ship strikes rock when Langman abandons his post and disappears below deck to get a drink of water.

The destruction of the *Nottingham Galley* is described in mainly sonic terms, Roberts once again exercising his impressive ability to invoke maritime sound for dramatic effect.

Once on the island, Roberts cleaves conscientiously to the original narratives for incident. The pace slows down and each chapter takes the form of a single day on Boon Island. Roberts excels at writing of physical attrition and environmental hazard. Roberts understands the cold. He writes brilliantly about the terrible and beautiful conjoined and kinetic properties of winter and the ocean. He knows how to communicate physical suffering. His immaculate research fills in the gaps left by the Deane brothers and Christopher Langman. He tells the reader how a cutlass could be converted into a saw. He speculates on how the survivors might have made a cap out of a seagull's skin. He communicates the details of building a boat and a raft better than the men that observed it firsthand had managed to do. Roberts had done an enormous amount of research. He visited Boon Island itself in order to verify certain details that seemed far-fetched in the original accounts. Yet the narrative teeters constantly on the brink of Roberts the researcher breaking into his own story in order to tell the reader how much he knows about the period and the conditions he is writing about. Roberts' research is seldom wielded lightly and constantly wars for the reader's attention with the rhythms and the static and dynamic tensions of good storytelling. At times *Boon Island* reads more like a survival manual than an actual novel.

Yet, despite the premium he places on research, Roberts makes some strange changes to the known facts. He invents an extra brother for John Deane as a crew member and gives him epilepsy. He removes Jasper Deane from the shipwreck altogether. He substitutes the younger Whitworth for the elder Whitworth. Roberts seems unaware that John Deane originally hailed from Nottingham, citing his place of origin as Twickenham instead. He gives the *Nottingham Galley* oars, seemingly mistaking it for a more traditional galleon.

People seem to elude Kenneth Roberts. His characters are ciphers. Christopher Langman is a pathetic, lazy, self-serving ingrate. Once marooned on Boon Island, Langman's threat is neutered and his narrative function is to contradict Deane as loudly and erroneously as possible. But Kenneth Roberts does something to Langman that even John and Jasper Deane refrained from doing. Roberts removes Langman's one impressive piece of moral high ground, his initial refusal to eat human flesh. Langman's abstinence is dismissed as religious primitivism. Langman believes the soul still resides in the flesh. He won't eat anything with a soul in it. Deane's religious faith is more enlightened and pragmatic. The man is dead. The soul is gone. The flesh is meat. If the men don't eat the meat then they will die. Deane is barely conflicted about the decision. The central dramatic act in Langman and Deane's story was the decision to revert to cannibalism. Kenneth Roberts botches his ace by refusing to allow his protagonists any ambiguity about what, in reality, must have been the most grievous decision either man ever had to make.

In terms of vitality and relative human complexity, *Boon Island's* main exception is Swede Butler. Swede is the most vibrant character in the novel. He is a force of nature. He is funny. He is likeably opinionated. He rebukes the crew for naivety. He argues with Langman. He even argues with Deane and in doing so succeeds in making Deane seem a bit more human.

John Deane is virtuous, pious and more than capable in a crisis. He is seldom wrong about anything. As a dramatist, Kenneth Roberts seems to miss the point of John Deane entirely. Deane's paradoxes and contradictions make him interesting. In *Boon Island* there is never any question that there might even be the trace elements of something true in Christopher Langman's complaints against Deane. In *Boon Island*, John Deane's unquestioned virtuousness and virtuosity becomes boring after a while. Only towards the end of the novel, when Deane is wilting under the effects of the cold, exhaustion and starvation, does he exhibit any real form of vulnerability. Only in New England, while convalescing in Jethro Furber's house, does John Deane finally become interesting. While observing Furber's children during dinner time Deane catches himself wondering what it would be like to eat them. It proves to be the only real interior conflict Deane experiences in the entire novel and comes far too late in the narrative to be of any real dramatic use.

The epilogue is largely botched. Any drama that might have been gleaned from Langman's visit to the magistrate is neutered by the fact that the whole of Portsmouth believes John Deane. Langman is virtually drummed out of New England. Miles Whitworth and Neal Butler are offered jobs by the locals. Deane is also offered employment but knows that Langman intends to make trouble for him back in London. Deane prepares to return to England and fight for his reputation.

The postscript informs the reader that John Deane defended his reputation so well that he was offered the position of consul for the port of Flanders and Ostend. There is no mention of his time in Russia or his work as a spy.

Index

If you enjoyed this book, you may also be interested in…

The Devil Comes to Dartmoor: The Haunting True Story of Mary Howard, Devon's 'Demon Bride'
Laura Quigley

The true story of the notorious Mary Howard, accused of murdering her four husbands, and of her lover, George Cutteford. Gathered from the varying historical accounts and including primary material comes this haunting tale of love, treachery and revenge in seventeenth-century Devon.

978 0 7524 6111 3

Notorious Blasted Rascal
Linda Strattman

The venal and depraved reputation of Colonel Francis Charteris (1672-1732) became legendary and long survived his death. In *Notorious Blasted Rascal*, Linda Stratmann tells the remarkable story of Charteris, and how his servant girl successfully prosecuted the notorious aristocratic rake for rape.

978 0 7509 4812 8

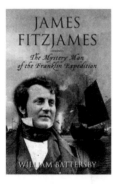

James Fitzjames: the Mystery Man of the Franklin Expedition
William Battersby

James Fitzjames was a hero of the early nineteenth-century Royal Navy. When he joined the Franklin Expedition he thought he would make his name. But instead the expedition completely disappeared and he never returned. Its fate is one of history's last great unsolved mysteries, as were the origins and background of James Fitzjames – until now.

978 0 7524 5512 9

Visit our website and discover thousands of other History Press books.

www.thehistorypress.co.uk

The History Press